LIGUORI CATHOLIC BIBLE STUDY

Letters
to the Romans
and Galatians

RECONCILING THE OLD AND NEW COVENANTS

WILLIAM A. ANDERSON, DMIN, PHD

Liguori
LIGUORI, MISSOURI

Imprimi Potest:
Harry Grile, CSsR, Provincial
Denver Province, The Redemptorists

Nihil Obstat: Rev. Msgr. Kevin Michael Quirk, JCD, JV
        Censor Liborum

Imprimatur: + Michael J. Bransfield
            Bishop of Wheeling-Charleston [West Virginia]
November 14, 2012

Published by Liguori Publications
Liguori, Missouri 63057

To order, call 800-325-9521
www.liguori.org

Copyright © 2013 William A. Anderson

All rights reserved. No part of this publication may be reproduced, stored in a retrieval system, or transmitted in any form or by any means—electronic, mechanical, photocopy, recording, or any other—except for brief quotations in printed reviews, without the prior written permission of Liguori Publications.

Cataloging-in-Publication Data on file with the Library of Congress

p ISBN 9780764821257
e ISBN 9780764823053

Scripture texts in this work are taken from the *New American Bible*, revised edition © 2010, 1991, 1986, 1970 Confraternity of Christian Doctrine, Washington, D.C., and are used by permission of the copyright owner. All Rights Reserved. No part of the *New American Bible* may be reproduced in any form without permission in writing from the copyright owner.

Liguori Publications, a nonprofit corporation, is an apostolate of The Redemptorists. To learn more about The Redemptorists, visit Redemptorists.com.

Printed in the United States of America
17 16 15 14 13 / 5 4 3 2 1
First Edition

Contents

NOTE: The length of each Bible section varies. Group leaders should combine sections as needed to fit the number of sessions in their program.

Dedication

This series is lovingly dedicated to the memory of my parents, Kathleen and Angor Anderson, in gratitude for all they shared with all who knew them, especially my siblings and me.

Acknowledgments

Bible studies and reflections depend on the help of others who read the manuscript and make suggestions. I am especially indebted to Sister Anne Francis Bartus, CSJ, DMin, whose vast experience and knowledge were very helpful in bringing this series to its final form.

Introduction to
Liguori Catholic Bible Study

READING THE BIBLE can be daunting. It's a complex book, and many a person of goodwill has tried to read the Bible and ended up putting it down in utter confusion. It helps to have a companion, and *Liguori Catholic Bible Study* is a solid one. Over the course of this series, you'll learn about biblical messages, themes, personalities, and events and understand how the books of the Bible rose out of the need to address new situations.

Across the centuries, people of faith have asked, "Where is God in this moment?" Millions of Catholics look to the Bible for encouragement in their journey of faith. Wisdom teaches us not to undertake Bible study alone, disconnected from the Church that was given Scripture to share and treasure. When used as a source of prayer and thoughtful reflection, the Bible comes alive.

Your choice of a Bible-study program should be dictated by what you want to get out of it. One goal of *Liguori Catholic Bible Study* is to give readers greater familiarity with the Bible's structure, themes, personalities, and message. But that's not enough. This program will also teach you to use Scripture in your prayer. God's message is as compelling and urgent today as ever, but we get only part of the message when it's memorized and stuck in our heads. It's meant for the entire person—physical, emotional, and spiritual.

We're baptized into life with Christ, and we're called to live more fully with Christ today as we practice the values of justice, peace, forgiveness, and community. God's new covenant was written on the hearts of the people of Israel; we, their spiritual descendants, are loved that intimately by God today. *Liguori Catholic Bible Study* will draw you closer to God, in whose image and likeness we are fashioned.

Group and Individual Study

The *Liguori Catholic Bible Study* series is intended for group and individual study and prayer. This series gives you the tools to start a study group. Gathering two or three people in a home or announcing the meeting of a Bible-study group in a parish or community can bring surprising results. Each lesson in this series contains a section to help groups study, reflect, pray, and share biblical reflections. Each lesson also has a second section for individual study.

Many people who want to learn more about the Bible don't know where to begin. This series gives them a place to start and helps them continue until they're familiar with all the books of the Bible.

Bible study can be a lifelong project, always enriching those who wish to be faithful to God's Word. When people complete a study of the whole Bible, they can begin again, making new discoveries with each new adventure into the Word of God.

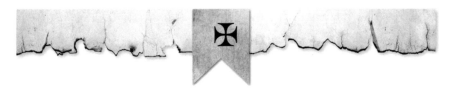

Lectio Divina
(Sacred Reading)

BIBLE STUDY isn't just a matter of gaining intellectual knowledge of the Bible; it's also about gaining a greater understanding of God's love and concern for creation. The purpose of reading and knowing the Bible is to enrich our relationship with God. God loves us and gave us the Bible to illustrate that love. As Pope Benedict XVI reminds us, a study of the Bible is not only an intellectual pursuit but also a spiritual adventure that should influence our dealings with God and neighbor.

The Meaning of *Lectio Divina*

Lectio divina is a Latin expression that means "divine or sacred reading." The process for *lectio divina* consists of Scripture readings, reflection, and prayer. Many clergy, religious, and laity use *lectio divina* in their daily spiritual reading to develop a closer and more loving relationship with God. Learning about Scripture has as its purpose the living of its message, which demands a period of reflection on the Scripture passages.

Prayer and *Lectio Divina*

Prayer is a necessary element for the practice of *lectio divina*. The entire process of reading and reflecting is a prayer. It's not merely an intellectual pursuit; it's also a spiritual one. Page 20 includes an Opening Prayer for gathering one's thoughts before moving on to the passages in each section. This prayer may be used privately or in a group. For those who use the book for daily spiritual reading, the prayer for each section may be repeated each day. Some may wish to keep a journal of each day's meditation.

Pondering the Word of God

Lectio divina is the ancient Christian spiritual practice of reading the holy Scriptures with intentionality and devotion. This practice helps Christians center themselves and descend to the level of the heart to enter an inner quiet space, finding God.

This sacred reading is distinct from reading for knowledge or information, and it's more than the pious practice of spiritual reading. It is the practice of opening ourselves to the action and inspiration of the Holy Spirit. As we intentionally focus on and become present to the inner meaning of the Scripture passage, the Holy Spirit enlightens our minds and hearts. We come to the text willing to be influenced by a deeper meaning that lies within the words and thoughts we ponder.

In this space, we open ourselves to be challenged and changed by the inner meaning we experience. We approach the text in a spirit of faith and obedience as a disciple ready to be taught by the Holy Spirit. As we savor the sacred text, we let go of our usual control of how we expect God to act in our lives and surrender our hearts and consciences to the flow of the divine (*divina*) through the reading (*lectio*).

The fundamental principle of *lectio divina* leads us to understand the profound mystery of the Incarnation, "The Word became flesh," not only in history but also within us.

Praying *Lectio* Today

Before you begin, relax your body and maintain a posture of prayer (back straight, eyes shut, feet flat on the floor). Then practice these four simple actions:

1. Read a passage from Scripture or the daily Mass readings. This is known as *lectio*. (If the Word of God is read aloud, the hearers listen attentively.)

2. Pray the selected passage with attention as you listen for a specific meaning that comes to mind. Once again, the reading is listened to or silently read and reflected or meditated on. This is known as *meditatio*.

3. The exercise becomes active. Pick a word, sentence, or idea that surfaces from your consideration of the chosen text. Does the reading remind you of a person, place, or experience? If so, pray about it. Compose your thoughts and reflection into a simple word or phrase. This prayer-thought will help you remove distractions during the *lectio*. This exercise is called *oratio*.

4. In silence, with your eyes closed, quiet yourself and become conscious of your breathing. Let your thoughts, feelings, and concerns fade as you consider the selected passage in the previous step (*oratio*). If you're distracted, use your prayer word to help you return to silence. This is *contemplatio*.

This exercise can take as long as you want, but in the context of this Bible study, 10 to 20 minutes should be sufficient.

Many teachers of prayer call contemplation the prayer of resting in God, a prelude to losing oneself in the presence of God. Scripture is transformed in our hearing as we pray and allow our hearts to unite intimately with the Lord. The Word truly takes on flesh, and this time it is manifested in our flesh.

How to Use This Bible-Study Companion

THE BIBLE, along with the commentaries and reflections found in this study, will help participants become familiar with the Scripture texts and lead them to reflect more deeply on the texts' message. At the end of this study, participants will have a firm grasp of the Letters to the Romans and Galatians and realize how these letters offer spiritual nourishment. This study is not only an intellectual adventure, it's also a spiritual one. The reflections lead participants into their own journey with the Scripture readings.

Context

When the author wrote the Letters to the Romans and Galatians, he didn't simply link random stories about the community—but rather, placed them in a context that often stressed a message. To help readers learn about each passage in relation to those around it, each lesson begins with an overview that puts the Scripture passages into context.

NOTE: Scripture texts in this work are taken from the *New American Bible,* revised edition © 2010, 1991, 1986, 1970 Confraternity of Christian Doctrine, Washington, D.C. and are used by permission of the copyright owner. All Rights Reserved. No part of the *New American Bible* may be reproduced in any form without permission in writing from the copyright owner.

Part 1: Group Study

To give participants a comprehensive study of the Letters to the Romans and Galatians, the book is divided into seven lessons. Lesson 1 is group study only; Lessons 2 through 7 are divided into Part 1, group study, and Part 2, individual study. For example, Lesson 2 covers passages from Romans 2 through 5. The study group reads and discusses only Romans 2 through 3:20 (Part 1). Participants privately read and reflect on Romans 3:21 through 5 (Part 2).

Group study may or may not include *lectio divina*. With *lectio divina*, the group meets for ninety minutes using the format on pages 17 and 18. Without *lectio divina*, the group meets for one hour using the format on page 17, and participants are urged to privately read the *lectio divina* section at the end of Part 1. It contains additional reflections on the Scripture passages studied during the group session that will take participants even further into the passages.

Part 2: Individual Study

The Scripture passages not covered in Part 1 are divided into two to six shorter components, one to be studied each day. Participants who don't belong to a study group can use the lessons for private sacred reading. They may choose to reflect on one Scripture passage per day, making it possible for a clearer understanding of the Scripture passages used in their *lectio divina* (sacred reading).

A PROCESS FOR SACRED READING

Liguori Publications has designed this study to be user friendly and manageable. However, group dynamics and leaders vary. We're not trying to keep the Holy Spirit from working in your midst, thus we suggest you decide beforehand which format works best for your group. If you have limited time, you could study the Bible as a group and save prayer and reflection for personal time.

However, if your group wishes to digest and feast on sacred Scripture through both prayer and study, we recommend you spend closer to ninety minutes each week by gathering to study and pray with Scripture. *Lectio divina* (see page 11) is an ancient contemplative prayer form that moves readers from the head to the heart in meeting the Lord. We strongly suggest using this prayer form whether in individual or group study. Below are two suggested formats:

GROUP-STUDY FORMATS

1. Bible Study

About one hour of group study

- ✠ Gathering and opening prayer (3 to 5 minutes)
- ✠ Read the Scripture passage aloud (5 minutes)
- ✠ Silently read the commentary and prepare to discuss it (3 to 5 minutes)
- ✠ Discuss the Scripture passage along with the commentary and reflections (40 minutes)
- ✠ Closing prayer (3 to 5 minutes)

2. Bible Study With *lectio divina*

About ninety minutes of group study

- ✠ Gathering and opening prayer (3 to 5 minutes)

✠ Read the Scripture passage aloud for the first time (5 minutes)

✠ Silently review the commentary and prepare to discuss it (3 to 5 minutes)

✠ Discuss the Scripture passage along with the commentary and reflection (30 minutes)

✠ Read the Scripture passage aloud a second time and allow some quiet time for meditation and contemplation (5 minutes)

✠ Spend time in prayer with the selected passage. Group participants will slowly read the Scripture passage a third time in silence, listening for the voice of God as they read. (10 to 20 minutes)

✠ Shared reflection (10 to 15 minutes)

✠ Closing prayer (3 to 5 minutes)

To become acquainted with lectio divina, *see page 11.*

Notes to the Leader

✠ Bring a copy of the *New American Bible,* revised edition.

✠ Plan which sections will be covered each week of your Bible Study.

✠ Read the material in advance of each session.

✠ Establish written ground rules. (Example: We will not keep you longer than ninety minutes; don't dominate the sharing by arguing or debating, etc.)

✠ Meet in an appropriate and welcoming gathering space (church building, meeting room, house).

✠ Provide name tags and perhaps use a brief icebreaker for the first meeting; ask participants to introduce themselves.

✠ Mark the Scripture passage(s) that will be read during the session.

✠ Decide how you would like the Scripture to be read aloud (whether by one or multiple readers).

✠ Use a clock or watch.

✠ Provide extra Bibles (or copies of the Scripture passages) for participants who don't bring their Bible.

✠ Ask participants to read "Introduction: Letters to the Romans and Galatians" (page 21) before the first session.

✠ Tell participants which passages to study and urge them to read the passages and commentaries before the meeting.

✠ If you use the *lectio divina* format, familiarize yourself with this prayer form ahead of time.

Notes to Participants

✠ Bring a copy of the *New American Bible,* revised edition.

✠ Read "Introduction: Letters to the Romans and Galatians" (page 21) before the first class.

✠ Read the Scripture passages and commentary before each session.

✠ Be prepared to share and listen respectfully. (This is not a time to debate beliefs or argue.)

Opening Prayer

Leader: O God, come to my assistance,

Response: O Lord, make haste to help me.

Leader: Glory be the Father, and to the Son, and to the Holy Spirit...

Response: ...as it was in the beginning, is now, and ever shall be, world without end. Amen.

Leader: Christ is the vine and we are the branches. As branches linked to Jesus, the vine, we are called to recognize that the Scriptures are always being fulfilled in our lives. It is the living Word of God living on in us. Come, Holy Spirit, fill the hearts of your faithful, and kindle in us the fire of your divine wisdom, knowledge, and love.

Response: Open our minds and hearts as we study your great love for us as shown in the Bible.

Reader: (Open your Bible to the assigned Scripture(s) and read in a paced, deliberate manner. Pause for one minute, listening for that word, phrase, or image that you may use in your *lectio divina* practice.)

Closing Prayer

Leader: Let us pray as Jesus taught us.

Response: Our Father...

Leader: Lord, inspire us with your Spirit as we study your Word in the Bible. Be with us this day and every day as we strive to know you and serve you and to love as you love. We believe that through your goodness and love, the Spirit of the Lord is truly upon us. Allow the words of the Bible, your Word, to capture us and inspire us to live as you live and to love as you love.

Response: Amen.

Leader: May the divine assistance remain with us always.

Response: In the name of the Father, and of the Son, and of the Holy Spirit. Amen.

INTRODUCTION

Letters to the Romans and Galatians

Read this overview before the first class.

WHEN A SMALL Bible study group was discussing the letters of Paul the Apostle, a woman in the group named Carol told the story of how a letter from a person she had never met changed her life. Two years prior to receiving the letter, her three-year-old son was killed when he ran in front of a speeding car. A few months after the accident, her husband, who appeared to be in good health, awoke one morning, told her that he felt "strange," and suddenly died of a heart attack. And just three months after her husband's death, she became so depressed that she decided she would end her life quietly at home. The woman prepared a short note to her sister and left it on a desk in her house, telling her sister that life had become too lonely and difficult. The day she chose to die, she purchased several bottles of sleeping pills and planned on taking them at bedtime. But, on her way home from the pharmacy, she picked up her mail and found a letter from a nun she had never met.

In her letter, the nun wrote that a friend who knew Carol asked the nun to pray for her, explaining the tragedies Carol experienced. The nun further explained that she was praying one day when she suddenly felt a strong urge to write Carol a letter. In the letter, the nun encouraged her to be strong, stressing that Jesus suffered a great deal and was later raised from the dead. "Unfortunately," the nun wrote, "many people stop at the death of Jesus and never enter into union with his resurrection." She went on to stress that Jesus knows suffering, but Jesus also knows resurrection. The nun added that Carol's son and husband were sharing in resurrection, and she noted that Carol had a different kind of resurrection to face at this time, namely a resurrection of spirit that would enable her to go on living for her lost family. The nun promised to continue to pray for Carol.

Carol told the study group that this letter opened her eyes to the foolishness of ending her life. She explained that the thoughts expressed in the letter helped her but—even more—the idea that a stranger would write to her with such love and concern touched her. The love expressed in it had such a deep effect on her that she sat and wept as she had never wept before. An hour later, she felt as though she had wept out all her bitterness and anger toward God and was ready to begin to live again. Due to this extraordinary event in Carol's life, she immediately flushed the sleeping pills down the drain, tore up the letter to her sister, and began to clean her house, something she hadn't done since her husband's death.

A letter of encouragement can make a great difference in our lives. This was also true for early Christian communities.

The Letters of Paul

Although fourteen of the twenty-one letters found in the New Testament have been attributed to Paul, most scholars agree that some of them were not written by him but instead by his disciples who believed that they were writing in the spirit of Paul and remained faithful to his message. Seven of the letters that are widely accepted to have been written by Paul are Romans, Corinthians 1 and 2, Galatians, Philippians, Thessalonians 1, and Philemon. Scholars agree that Romans and Galatians, which we address in this book, were without a doubt authored by Paul. In this Catholic Bible study series, distinctions will be made between the letters written by Paul and those likely penned by another author that have been frequently attributed to Paul through the centuries.

Through his letters, Paul applied Jesus' life and message to the Church.

He addressed issues that became dominant in the Church after Jesus' ascension. Each letter addresses particular issues and arguments within the community to whom he was writing. Though it was not Paul's intention to present a systematic theology, his writings do include a large number of theological insights that have greatly influenced the theology of the Church down to our present age.

In the New Testament, the letters of the Pauline corpus are assembled in descending order according to their length, ranging from Romans to Philemon (longest to shortest). Romans stands as one of the most significant of Paul's letters due to its length. This letter exhorts about God's righteousness and love that come to us through Jesus Christ. Like the nun in the opening story, Paul wrote his letters with love and concern for the communities to which he sent them. As the early Church often had conflicts arise, the letters helped these communities to work through divisions and act lovingly toward one another.

Paul's Conflict With Jewish Christians

The theme of Paul's Letters to the Romans and Galatians would come as no surprise to those who are familiar with Paul's mission to the Gentiles. If news reporters were to write about Paul today, they would call him an activist who was driven to dedicate himself totally to whatever cause he believed to be true and important. When we first meet Paul in the Acts of the Apostles, we encounter a totally energetic and dedicated Jew. He strongly believed that the followers of Jesus were contaminating Judaism. Like many pious Jews, he most likely thought that God would punish the Jews for allowing this new sect to flourish, so he dedicated himself to eradicating it—that is Christianity. Paul didn't wait for them to come to him or to the area where he lived; but rather, he went out of his way to find and persecute Christians. Nothing would stand in the way of what he believed to be important.

The Acts of the Apostles tells us that Paul was on a journey to Damascus with papers allowing him to arrest Christians and have them cast into jail. On his journey, a dazzling light blinded him and the voice of Christ asked Paul why he was persecuting him. In this vision, Christ identified himself with Christians. But when the vision ended, Paul was blind and had to be led by hand to Damascus where he fasted for three days until a disciple named Ananias was sent by the Lord to baptize him.

Ananias announced that Paul was an instrument of the Lord to bring Christ's message to the Gentiles (9:1–19). As a result of this experience, Paul abandoned his persecution of Christians and directed his tireless and heroic energies toward spreading Christ's message. Paul could now say he no longer lived for himself but instead for Christ. His plight became one of great suffering for Christ, even to the point of dying in his efforts to share Jesus' message.

As Paul preached about Christ, he converted many from among the Gentiles. In his endeavors to bring the Gentiles to Christ, he recognized how difficult it was for them to follow the Jewish laws and practices, especially circumcision. Thus his mission to them eventually led him to fight for exemption from Jewish laws and practices for Gentile converts. This would prove to be a difficult task, since many Jewish converts to Christ believed that the Gentiles had to convert to Judaism in order to become disciples of Christ.

When Paul and Barnabas completed their first missionary journey, they traveled to Jerusalem for a meeting which some would identify as the Jerusalem Council, the first council of the Church. In the Acts of the Apostles, we learn that Barnabas is the disciple who welcomed Paul into the early community when others were uncertain about the sincerity of Paul's conversion. Barnabas trusted Paul and became a missionary to the Gentiles along with him. For this reason, Barnabas joined Paul in going to Jerusalem to meet with the Church leaders concerning the demands placed on the Gentile converts.

At the time when Paul and Barnabas traveled to Jerusalem, the Jewish followers of Jesus who believed that Jesus was the Christ were known as "the Way," a title used to signify the new way of living as a faithful Jew. The Jewish converts who accepted Jesus as the Christ expected many other Jews to eventually join them, believing that Judaism would now continue with the long-awaited Messiah. The rapid and unexpected spread of faith in Christ among the Gentiles brought many Jewish Christians into conflict with Paul and Barnabas, who now had to travel to Jerusalem to plead the cause of the Gentile converts.

Leaders of "the Way" met with Paul and Barnabas to discuss the Gentile converts' place among the followers of Christ. They brought exciting news to the council about the number of converts from among the Gentiles but had to address the practice of circumcision that was a stumbling block for the new converts. However, Paul eventually persuaded the Christian leaders in Jerusalem to allow the Gentiles to convert without adhering to the dictates of the Mosaic Law.

Acts of the Apostles sets the scene for a major conflict that hounded Paul during his missionary endeavors. We read: "Some who had come down from Judea were instructing the brothers, 'Unless you are circumcised according to the Mosaic practice, you cannot be saved'" (Acts 15:1). An apparently heated discussion took place at the council, but the verdict eventually was sent to the Christians at Antioch declaring: "It is the decision of the holy Spirit and of us not to place on you any burden beyond these necessities, namely to abstain from meats of strangled animals, and from unlawful marriage" (Acts 15:28). Circumcision was not mentioned as one of the necessities, thus freeing the Gentile converts from this practice.

As often happens after councils, there were some who refused to accept the decision of the Church council. Many Jewish Christians continued to preach that Gentiles had to be circumcised when they wished to become a Christian. These followers came to be known as Judaizers, a group of rigid Christian Jews who refused to abandon Mosaic Law and practices and attempted to impose them on new followers of Christ. Paul's message about freedom from the Mosaic Law infuriated the Judaizers, so they often tried to undermine him and his teachings. Thus, they plagued Paul often during his missions to the point that he was no longer able to preach in their synagogues.

Paul himself continued to protest that his Jewish heritage and practices were sacred to him, but he also believed that the Mosaic Law had lost its force and should no longer be a condition for being a Christian.

Surprisingly, Paul's greatest enemies were not those who rejected Jesus as the Messiah but those who accepted that Jesus was the Messiah and who also believed that following the Mosaic Law was necessary for a true conversion. When Paul attempted to preach that circumcision and some practices of the Mosaic Law were no longer necessary to enforce for the Gentile Christians, he encountered rejection and persecution at the hands of Jewish Christians.

Romans and Galatians

Studying the Letters to the Romans and the Galatians in a single volume is a logical approach to understanding the meaning contained therein. Though Paul wrote both letters at a different time in his ministry and treats his audience differently, the themes found in both letters are similar to each other. For example, in both letters Paul writes about the pre-eminence of faith in Jesus over the works of the Israelite Law. Also, it is good to note that Paul's Letter to the Galatians comes later in our current biblical format, but it was actually written before his Letter to the Romans.

The conflict between Paul and the Judaizers became a central point for both of these letters. In his Letter to the Romans, Paul speaks more calmly than he does to Galatia. And while his letter to the church in Rome appears to be more like an essay than a letter, his Letter to the Galatians speaks more pointedly and harshly about faith and works. Due to these shared themes, the commentary and reflections for these two letters were compiled together in this volume of the *Liguori Catholic Bible Study* series.

The author of Acts of the Apostles tells us that the Jews at Jerusalem entice the authorities to arrest Paul. When Paul appeals to Rome, he is later sent as a prisoner in chains there. Paul wrote his Letter to the Romans before his journey to Jerusalem, and this took place more than two years before he was taken to Rome as a prisoner. He planned to go to Rome as a free man, but circumstances in Jerusalem led him to be brought to Rome in chains. It is believed that Paul was beheaded in Rome under the Christian persecution of Nero, around the year 64.

Authorship of Romans and Galatians

Because the Letter to the Romans clearly expresses Paul's ideology and style, no one has ever seriously doubted that he was indeed the author. Paul apparently had time to reflect on and plan carefully what he wished to say, as his Letter to the Romans is more peaceful, measured, and rational than his Letter to the Galatians. Although the message is similar to that of the Galatians, here he is writing to a Christian community founded by other missionaries. Most of the Roman Christians did not know Paul personally, although they may have heard about him. Thus, he likely wished to ingratiate himself with his audience, but at the same time he remained faithful to the theme that salvation comes through faith in Jesus Christ and not through works of the law.

Likewise, almost all commentators agree that Paul is certainly the author of the Letter to the Galatians. This letter has his strength of style and language, and it speaks with the authority of one who knows the members of the audience to whom he is writing. Ancient writers also state that Paul authored this letter.

Paul's Letter to the Romans

Some commentators refuse to place Romans under the heading of a "letter." They consider a letter to be a form of communication intended for a person or persons who are separated from each other, and not intended to be addressed to the general public. Paul's Letter to the Romans is more like an essay that presents Paul's theological and practical views in a more subdued and restrained manner than is found in some of his other letters. It is certainly his longest letter and most likely his last letter, at least among the letters known to be written by Paul.

The Roman Audience

With the exception of his epistle to the Christian community at Rome, Paul wrote all his letters to communities he founded. It is noteworthy that Paul never visited Rome until he was brought there in chains, but he learned about the faith and concerns of the community through reports from others who had been there. This indicates he knew some Christians who were living in Rome when he wrote his letter. At the letter's end, he greets Prises and Aquila, whom he describes as "my co-workers in Christ Jesus" (Romans 16:3). He also sends greetings to others who are living in Rome. The reality that he knew so many people likely indicates that a sizable number of Christians lived there.

Paul shows his concern for all Christians in his letter, including both those he never met along with those he knew. And he was fully aware of the problems and conflicts of the Christians in Rome. In his letter, he shares with them his insights about Christ and Christianity as they developed through his years of preaching about Jesus. Years later, when Paul was brought to Rome as a prisoner, many of these converts to Christianity greeted him there.

The situation among Christians in Rome came about through changing situations in Rome itself. The Jewish converts to Christ were most likely the original group who brought the message of Jesus to Rome. During the time of the apostles, there were Jewish converts to Christianity, and these converts believed strongly that those who accepted Jesus as the Messiah must also accept Jewish laws and rituals. Converts from among the Jews were not the only ones to follow Christ in the first century, as there were also many Gentiles who began to believe in Jesus as the Messiah.

Bitter conflicts between Jews who accepted Jesus as the Messiah and those who did not developed in Rome and peaked around the year 49. A Roman historian named Suetonius wrote that Emperor Claudius, as a result of this conflict among the Jews, issued an edict expelling all Jews from Rome. According to Suetonius, the Jews were all to be banished because of their relationship to a certain "Chrestus," which obviously pointed to Jesus Christ. Since the Romans could not distinguish between Jews who accepted Jesus as the Christ and those who did not, the edict affected them all.

Around the year 54, at the death of Claudius, Nero became emperor and allowed the Jews to return to Rome. With the return of the Jews to the city, a different type of conflict arose. The Gentiles spent more than four years free of the Jewish Christians who wanted to impose Jewish laws and rituals on the Gentile converts to Christianity. A clash of belief took place as both sides remained adamant in resisting each other. The Gentile Christians not only refused to follow the Jewish laws and rituals, but they began to look down upon the Mosaic Law and saw it as unnecessary. So it was this conflict that Paul addressed in his Letter to the Romans.

Date of the Epistle

Although Paul's Letter to the Romans comes first in the canonical presentation of the New Testament letters, it is not the first letter written by Paul. Paul wrote his Letter to the Romans from Greece, likely Corinth, between the years 56 and 58 (see Acts 20:2–3). The dating of the epistle is based on circumstances found in the writing. As mentioned above, Emperor Claudius expelled all Jews from Rome around the year 49, but Paul sends greetings to two Jewish converts named Prisca and Aquila, who were expelled and returned after Nero became emperor.

Paul had long planned to move his mission further west to Spain, intending to stop at Rome on his journey. When he wrote to the Romans, he was about to go to Jerusalem with a collection for the Christians in the area who were struggling and in need of financial support. Throughout his missionary journeys among the Gentiles, Paul gathered contributions from Gentile converts. He hoped the collection would show the concern of the Gentile Christians for their brothers and sisters in Jerusalem and, at the same time, prove to the Jewish Christians there that he was faithful to the Jewish origins of faith in Jesus. He realized the dangers involved in his visit to Jerusalem, but he wanted to bring the collection to the Christians there himself rather than sending it with an envoy. The dangers he faced in Jerusalem eventually led to his imprisonment, as well as his later move to Rome in chains.

In Acts 20:3, we read that toward the end of his third missionary journey, with the collection ready to be brought to Jerusalem, Paul stopped in Greece for three months. Since Paul had a very successful mission at Corinth, he would most likely have stayed there. At the time, he was already preparing for another missionary journey after leaving the collection in Jerusalem, a journey that seemed to include Rome and Spain. Dating the letter from Paul's journey to Jerusalem would place the writing of this epistle around the year 57.

Outline of Romans

The Human Condition

After a brief introduction in which Paul identifies himself and his mission, he describes the human condition as it existed without Christ. Paul exhorts Jews and Gentiles alike to abandon idolatry and serve the living God. The Jews, who had been given the Mosaic Law, are told that they will be judged according to it, while the Gentiles will be judged according to the law existing within themselves. For Jews and Gentiles alike, it is the interior spirit that counts. Paul declares that all are under the bondage of sin.

Faith in Christ

Justification comes to the Jews and Gentiles, not as a result of law or knowledge, but as a result of faith. It is a gift, freely given by God through Jesus Christ. Because God chose Abraham and his descendants before the Law came into being, Paul uses Abraham as an example of justification by faith. For the Christian, justification comes from God through Christ. Just as death came through the offense of Adam and affected all people, so the gift of salvation came through one man, Jesus Christ, for the sake of all. This gift, which is not earned by any of us, comes as a result of faith.

Through baptism the Christian dies to sin and rises to new life in union with Jesus Christ. Instead of living under the power and slavery to sin, the Christian now lives as a slave to justice. This new life brings with it a spirit of adoption that makes the Christian an heir with Christ. All creation, subject to futility and struggle because of sin, now has a new hope for glory. The love of God for all enables Paul to proclaim that nothing in the world can separate us from this love.

God's Faithfulness

Although some might think otherwise, God is always faithful to the promises made to Israel. Just as God chose Israel as the Chosen People, God continues to choose Christians to be "children of God" (Romans 8:14). The mercy of God extends to the Gentiles because of their strong faith. Thus, God chooses a remnant, along with the patriarchs of old (the root of the Israelite nation), who will consecrate the whole of Israel. In remaining faithful to the promises made in the past, God will show mercy to the Israelites who have not earned these gifts, but who, like the Gentiles, receive them as pure gifts from God.

Paul reminds Christians that they belong to the Body of Christ and that they do not live for themselves; instead they must offer themselves as a living sacrifice to God. Paul calls them to love one another and their enemies, for love fulfills the law. This love leads the Christian to avoid scandalizing the weak, even if this means abstaining from those things that are allowed under the law. Christians are to live a life of perfect harmony and acceptance of one another.

Paul concludes his Letter to the Romans with a message about his travel plans and a greeting to those residing in Rome.

Paul's Letter to the Galatians

A candidate in a political primary campaign wrote about a visit to members of a particular group of workers who had a strong influence on the way many other members of that group voted. When he laid out his plan for the future development of the area, he received wide and open acceptance from the workers. He believed he had more realistic goals to offer than his opponent, who was scheduled to speak to the workers three days later. As he left the meeting, the candidate told one of his aides that they had the workers' votes "sewed up."

A week later, the candidate was shocked to read that the workers were leaning toward supporting his opponent in the primary. He called for an emergency meeting of his aides, angry that he had apparently lost the opportunity to convince the workers of the help he wished to offer them. In the space of only three days, his voters had been influenced to change their stance in favor of his opponent. The aides advised the candidate to call the leader of these workers, express his surprise and disappointment, and offer to meet with him and the group once again to answer any questions or concerns that must have arisen during this time. Because this block of votes was so important, the candidate was willing to cancel all other engagements in the area to meet with them at their convenience.

The eventual outcome of this call was an invitation to have both candidates come to a meeting to respond to questions from the floor. The importance of these voters left the candidates with little choice but to accept the invitation. For the candidate who called for a second hearing, this proved to be a successful move, as he was able to answer objections from his opponent and show how he was prepared to respond to the needs of the workers. The group of workers eventually gave him their endorsement.

In a sense, Paul the Apostle was always on a spiritual campaign for Jesus Christ. He had discovered a valuable gift in the person and message of Jesus Christ, and he wanted the world to share this gift. This desire became the driving force of his life and led him through dangers and hardships that he might have otherwise avoided. When he left the people of Galatia, he could look back with joy on their acceptance of the gospel message. But he soon heard that the Galatians, in a very short time, had changed their hearts regarding the message; and, like the candidate in the story above, Paul immediately contacted them. He wanted to reclaim them for Christ and his message.

The Galatian Audience

Although we have no doubt about the author of the letter, we do have some doubt about the specific audience for whom the letter was written. Originally, the area called Galatia included the north-central section of Asia Minor. In 25 BCE, Rome incorporated Galatia into a Roman province, which became the province of Galatia. At that time, it added to the territory a section south of old Galatia; the province of Galatia now included places such as Pisidia, Lystra, and Derbe, all of which are mentioned in the Acts of the Apostles.

It is difficult to determine whether the letter was written to the old

Galatia to the north or to the area of Galatia that also included sections to the south. Although we can say that Paul wrote his letter to the people of Galatia, we cannot state with certainty the exact audience for whom the letter was intended. The difficulty in naming the exact audience of the letter leaves us with a further difficulty in trying to establish exactly when it was written. During his first missionary journey, Paul visited Antioch in Pisidia (Acts 13:14), located in the southern portion of Galatia. During his second and third missionary journeys, he visited an area named in the Book of Acts as Galatia (16:6; 18:23). This reference to Galatia in Acts refers to the northern area of the province, or old Galatia.

If Paul wrote to the churches founded during his first missionary journey, he would have been writing to those in the southern portion of the province. This would date his letter somewhere around the year 49. If, however, he wrote this letter to the areas he visited during his second and third missionary journeys, then we would have to date the letter around the year 54. All we can say with certainty is that Paul wrote his letter somewhere between these two dates.

Paul's Occasion to Write to Galatia

Paul addresses his letter to the people he had converted from paganism on one of his missionary journeys. He writes about justification by faith in Jesus and not by works of the law (Galatians 2:16). He also confronts those who were teaching that freedom in Christ meant freedom to do whatever they wanted, including actions that were previously considered sinful. Paul teaches about the value of Christ's sacrifice on the cross and that Christians were free from the burdens of the Mosaic Law.

When he established the church in Galatia, he taught the converts about the superiority of faith in Christ over the Law, but after he left, the people accepted a different gospel as presented by the later arrival of the Judaizers. The Judaizers preached that practices and rituals of the Mosaic Law, including circumcision, should be added to Paul's message about Christ. Therefore, they challenged Paul's authority as an apostle, stating that he was not a companion of Jesus and that his message was contrary to that of the original disciples of Jesus. They accused Paul of not teaching the necessity of circumcision for salvation in Christ as well as other practices of the Mosaic Law.

Paul's aim in the letter was to lead the people back to his original teaching, which rejected the practice of the Mosaic Law and circumcision. His anger flared when he realized that the people he converted abandoned his message to follow the teachings of the Judaizers. This Letter to the church in Galatia has a tone of a parent who is rebuking and re-educating his or her children.

Outline of Galatians

Loyalty to the Gospel

Paul expresses his dismay that the Galatians have so easily abandoned the gospel he preached to them. He speaks boldly, asking if the people now think he is trying to gain favor with them or if he is speaking strongly for the sake of the gospel, no matter what they think about him.

Paul's Defense

Paul defends his teachings by reviewing his life before his conversion and showing that his teachings were approved by the church in Jerusalem. He declares that a person is justified, not by the Law of Moses, but by faith in Jesus.

Faith and Freedom

Paul becomes upset with the Galatians for their change of mind from the teachings he gave them. He taught them about the freedom from the Law of Moses which came with the fulfillment of the promise in the person of Jesus Christ. He warns his readers not to throw this freedom away.

Living as a Christian

Paul reminds his readers of the freedom which comes with faith in Christ. The freedom is not for impurity, but a freedom to live by the Spirit of God, avoiding every type of evil. Those who transgress should be cut off from the community for a period of time for the sake of their repentance. Paul writes the end of the letter in his own hand to prove that the words of the letter, which may be written by a scribe, are indeed his words.

The Righteousness of God

ROMANS 1

For, I am not ashamed of the gospel. It is the power of God for the salvation of everyone who believes: for Jew first, and then Greek (1:16).

Opening Prayer (SEE PAGE 20)

Context

Paul introduces himself to the Romans as an apostle chosen to preach the gospel of the Son of God, who is a descendant of the line of David. He praises the Romans for their faith and prays that he will somehow come to Rome, a visit he long desired to make. Since he knows there are Jewish and Gentile Christians in Rome, he declares that he is not ashamed of preaching the gospel to the Jews as well as Gentiles, as the gospel provides the power of God for the salvation of all. He believes that evidence of God can be known through creation, meaning that those who practice wickedness have no excuse; and while they may claim to be wise, they are actually fools. Furthermore, he has a stern warning for those who practice unnatural sexual behavior, declaring that those who do this are worthy of death.

GROUP STUDY (ROMANS 1)

Read aloud Romans 1.

1:1–7 Paul's Apostleship

Paul opens his epistle with the customary introduction used during his time. In accordance with this custom, he names the sender, the one to whom the letter is sent, and greets his audience. He names himself as the sender and calls himself a servant of Jesus Christ. In the Old Testament, the prophets spoke of themselves as servants, or slaves, of the Lord. This title identified God as so great that all people should see themselves as servants or slaves to God. Paul, like a slave, is ready to respond to any call from God.

Paul views himself as having a special call as an apostle who was set aside for preaching the gospel that God promised through the prophets. An apostle was one who witnessed and preached about the resurrection of Jesus. Paul believes that his vision of Christ on the road to Damascus makes him a witness of Christ's resurrection, therefore he views his call to be an apostle as stemming from a special act of God described in Acts. Though this call did not come to him in the same manner of other apostles called by the Lord during Jesus' life on earth, Paul believes himself to be an apostle called in a special manner on the road to Damascus. He fulfills part of this call by writing his Letter to the Romans.

When Paul writes of being set aside for "the gospel of God," the reader should keep in mind that Paul is not speaking of the written gospels as they are today. None of the four gospels were written when Paul preached, although many of the messages and sayings of Jesus were being preached by the close disciples of Jesus. For that reason, Paul must speak of the gospel of God promised previously through God's prophets in the Holy Scriptures, which would be a reference to the writings known to us as the Old Testament. For Paul, the prophets spoke of the Son of God, who descended from the line of David in the flesh, that is, as a human being. Linking Jesus with the line of David establishes Jesus' call as the Messiah. Through his resurrection from the dead, Jesus was then established as the Son of God in power when all in heaven, on earth, and below the earth can proclaim that Jesus Christ is Lord (see Philippians 2:6–11).

After naming himself sender of the letter and stating its theme, Paul finishes his greeting by naming those to whom the letter is addressed. He writes his letter to all the people of Rome who have accepted Jesus' message, addressing them as those called to "be saints." Paul uses the customary blessing found in Jewish letters of his day, but he adds the name of Jesus Christ to this blessing, thus making it a Christian blessing. He wishes his audience the blessings of grace and peace in their lives. This is the usual Jewish blessing, and it refers to a life filled with harmony and love in the presence of God.

1:8–15 Thanksgiving

The ordinary beginning of most letters of ancient times consisted of the greeting followed immediately by some type of thanksgiving. Paul directs his thanks to God through Jesus Christ for the faith of the Romans. The Romans' acceptance of the faith had apparently spread to the other Christian communities that Paul visited. Because many considered Rome to be the embodiment of the civilized world, the conversion of its citizens would be significant to all Christian people. Their conversion, and the depth of that conversion, seems to have been part of the message relayed to the other Christian communities. Paul is thankful for the word he has received about the faith of the Roman Christians.

Because Paul wishes the Romans to know of his concern for them, he informs them of his constant prayers for their welfare. Paul refers to his preaching of the gospel as a form of worship of God, on whom he calls to witness the truth of his concern for the Romans. He tells them that he is praying that God will allow him to visit with them. Later in the letter (15:24), we find that Paul has already made some tentative plans to visit the Romans on his way to Spain.

The reason Paul gives for wanting to visit with the Romans is to encourage them to live their faith and also for Paul to receive encouragement from them. He wishes to share some spiritual gift with them, namely his preaching about Jesus and a means to strengthen them in their faith. He does not see himself as one who plants, but he desires to harvest some fruit among them and as well as among all the Gentiles.

Paul stresses his longing to visit with them. This need to repeat his wish may arise from Paul's hope of being well-received by the Romans, as though he feared that his absence in the past may have led them to believe that he does not care about them. Paul stresses that he has been kept from visiting them up to this point. In the Acts of the Apostles, we learn that Paul and his companions wished to follow certain routes in their missionary travels, but the Spirit led them in other directions. Paul is referring to his need to follow the promptings of the Spirit, which, until now, have prevented him from turning his attention to Rome. He plays no favorites, but preaches to the Greeks and non-Greeks, and to the wise and the ignorant. He views his ministry as an obligation, perhaps a reference to his belief that he is indeed a slave of Jesus Christ. In order to fulfill his mission as he understands it, he longs to preach the gospel to them in Rome. Though he is called to all people in all places, Rome, as the center of the Gentile world, calls out to Paul in a special way.

1:16–17 God's Power for Salvation

In these two verses, Paul presents the central theme of his letter—the relationship between faith and salvation. Paul expresses that he feels no shame in presenting the gospel message to the entire world. The Jews believed that anyone who died on the cross was without doubt a criminal and was cursed. The Book of Deuteronomy speaks of the corpse of someone who is hanged on a tree and says: "You must bury it the same day; anyone who is hanged is a curse of God" (Deuteronomy 21:23). So many people would experience shame in preaching about a Messiah who suffered such a shameful death on a cross. Paul not only preached Jesus as crucified, but he knew he must convince his audience that Jesus' crucifixion brought salvation and was not a curse of God. To understand this, it is important to note that many good Jews would have been embarrassed to claim that they are followers of someone who died on a cross. Paul believes and teaches the contrary—that is that the power of salvation comes from the death and resurrection of Jesus.

He explains that the gospel contains the power of God, which leads all believers to salvation. Because the Jews were the first to be chosen by God, Paul sees this gift of the gospel reaching out to them first, and then to the Gentiles. He uses the term *Greeks* to signify all Gentile people. Throughout the letter, Paul talks about God's "righteousness," or justification (justice). The Greek word used in this letter is not easily translated into English. It includes a sense of relationship with God, an acceptance of the person that does not merit God's grace. Even if a person acts according to God's call to love, God owes that person nothing. The fact that blessings are shared with such a person is a pure gift from God. The very idea of "justification" is that it originates with God. The revelation of this gift of justification comes to us through the gospel, and is received through faith. Paul adapts a quotation from Habakkuk, an Old Testament prophet, who tells of God's protection for the person faithful to God (2:4). The one who lives according to this justice shall live by faith.

1:18–32 Punishment for Idolaters

As Paul prepares to speak about human depravity, he begins by stressing the wrath of God. This does not imply some imperfection in God, who seems to act with seething anger. Instead, Paul presents the image of God as seen through the eyes of the sinner. Just as the justice of God is revealed to those of faith, so the wrath of God is revealed to those who turn to idolatry. Paul realizes that Rome is also a center of idolatry, so his message addresses those who do not believe in Jesus as the Christ as well as those involved in pagan worship.

Paul stresses that the invisible truths about God can be known through the visible truths of creation. He is challenging those who claim that they have never heard about God or the ways of God. Sinners themselves have chosen to obstruct these truths through their sinful attitudes. Because these truths about God can be known through creation from the beginning of time, the Gentiles have no excuse for not praising or offering thanks to God. Because of their vanity, they are living in their own darkness. Paul believes they can know God through created gifts, but on their own accord they chose not to offer thanks and glory to God. In choosing to reject the

Creator for the sake of worshiping creatures, they live in the darkness of ignorance and evil. Sinners of every age believe that they are wise, but they are actually fools who worship images of human beings, birds, four-legged animals, or snakes. These images were often found in pagan worship in Rome and elsewhere in the Roman Empire during Paul's era.

As a result of their worship of created images, God abandons the un-believers to their own sinful punishment. For they worshiped creatures rather than the Creator, and therefore their sinfulness becomes their punishment. As a result, God allowed them to follow their corrupting and disgraceful ways. Paul refers to females as exchanging natural relations for unnatural and males performing acts with other males. Since these actions seem to be common and known to Paul and others, he could be referring to actions that took place in many of the fertility rights of the day as a form of pagan worship. He was most likely unaware of sexual orientations known in our day. Rumors of promiscuity in Rome circulated throughout the empire and could have become grotesque as the rumors passed from one village to the next.

As a result of sinfulness, Paul contends that pagans refused to recog-nize the true God, and they were not able to see the presence of God in creation. Paul gives a list of more than twenty sins that bring punishment on the people, among them greed, malice, envy, murder, rivalry, gossips, and ruthlessness. In Paul's day, preachers used lists of sins to express the depravity into which the people had fallen. Paul chooses to insert one of these lists here, which leads us to suspect that not all of the sins named at this point were actually being practiced as Paul states.

Paul again refuses to excuse sinners who reject God and who, he claims, are able to know God through creation. These sinners not only choose spiritual death for themselves but also applaud others who choose such a death. They are not responsible only for their own sinfulness but for leading others into sin and encouraging them. In this passage, Paul could be stressing a stereotype of the Gentiles that Jews often attributed to the way of life of unbelieving Gentiles.

Review Questions

1. What does Paul means when he says that Jesus is born Son of God in power through his resurrection?

2. Why is it important that Jesus is a descendant of David?

3. How are we slaves of Jesus Christ?

4. What does Paul mean when he speaks of the "power of God for the salvation of everyone" (Romans 1:16)?

5. If we had never been taught about God, how could we know about God from creation, as Paul states in Romans?

Closing Prayer (SEE PAGE 20)

Pray the closing prayer now or after *lectio divina*.

Lectio Divina (SEE PAGE 11)

Relax your body and maintain a posture of prayer (back straight, eyes shut, feet flat on the floor). This exercise can take as long as you want, but in the context of this Bible study, 10 to 20 minutes should be sufficient.

The meditations that follow are provided only to help group participants use this prayer form, but note that *lectio* is intended to bring one to a place of prayerful contemplation where the Word of God speaks to the hearer from his or her heart. See page 11 for further instruction.

1:1–7 Paul's Apostleship

Following the direction of Paul to the Gentiles, we also are called to view ourselves as servants of Jesus Christ. When Paul uses the image of "slave," he does this to assert that we are called to be willing slaves; not slaves who are owned by a master, but those who willingly choose to follow Christ. In this sense, we belong to another, namely Jesus Christ. Like Paul, we are chosen to be servants for Christ and one another.

In John's Gospel, Jesus tells his disciples, "It was not you who chose me, but I who chose you" (John 15:16). These words also apply to us today. As baptized Christians, we are dedicated to act as though we are servants of Christ in the world, willing to live Jesus' message in our life. Paul, as an apostle, offers himself to be used in whatever way Christ wishes. Christ would have us think and act in the same manner.

✠ *What can I learn from this passage?*

1:8–15 Thanksgiving

Paul recognizes our need for one another. As he gives thanks to God for the faithful, he notes that knowledge of faith in Christians at Rome has spread. Therefore, he encourages many others outside of Rome to practice faith as well. In so doing, he expresses a foundation for community life to encourage others in their faith as well as receive it in return from others. Just as he preached his message for the people of his own era, we can apply it to our life today. For we are called to encourage and receive encouragement and support from one another as we live our Christian lives.

✠ *What can I learn from this passage?*

1:16–17 God's Power for Salvation

Late one night, some friends of a teenager decided to vandalize school property in revenge for a principal's ruling that any student who was found in the school hallways during class time without a written excuse would have to remain after class. One teenager refused to vandalize the school with his friends, and when they accused him of being a coward, he simply answered, "I'm a Christian."

Like Paul and that teenager, we must never be ashamed of living the gospel of Jesus Christ. Paul reminds us that we are not living God's message on our own power or ingenuity, but with the help of God who brought us salvation through Jesus Christ. At times, we may seem to be preaching by living our faith openly, but we must live the gospel message, even in those moments when it takes great courage.

✠ *What can I learn from this passage?*

1:18–32 Punishment for Idolators

A young adult said that he envied people who did not believe in God, since they could enjoy many pleasures in life that were contrary to God's law without guilt and still have an opportunity to be saved. After all, people cannot be judged on what they do not know. But, Paul would not agree with this young man. He believes that all people can know about God's law through learning about it explicitly or through discovering it in God's creation. Christians know God's law through an understanding of the life and message of Jesus Christ. Living according to this knowledge is a light in the darkness of sin in the world. Christians have the call to become an example of Christ's message to the world so that those who lack faith in Christ may find that their suspicions about God's law as learned through creation are true.

✠ *What can I learn from this passage?*

INDIVIDUAL STUDY

This lesson does not have an individual-study component.

LESSON 2
Justification Through Faith
ROMANS 2—5

Therefore, since we have been justified by faith, we have peace with God through our Lord Jesus Christ, through whom we have gained access by faith to the peace in which we stand, and we boast in hope of the glory of God (5:1–2).

Opening Prayer (SEE PAGE 20)

Context

Part 1: Romans 2—3:20 Paul is confronting the antagonism between the Jewish and Gentile converts to Christianity, explaining that both are bound by law, but a different kind of law. Whether Jews or Gentiles, those who judge the other must be tested by the same judgment that they cast on others. Jews and Gentiles alike experience affliction for evil acts or glory and peace for the good that they do. All will be judged by what they know and accept, whether or not they adhere to the Law of Moses. However, Jews and Gentiles alike are called to follow the law that is written on their hearts and within their conscience. Paul's exhortation does not intend to break the Mosaic Law, but it does free the Gentiles from learning all of the rights and rituals that the Jews have adhered to throughout their faith lives.

The Mosaic Law brings knowledge of sin. In reality, a Jew who breaks the Mosaic Law is acting as though he is not circumcised, and the Gentile who is keeping God's commands is acting as though he is circumcised. The Jews have an advantage since they were entrusted with God's law. Regardless of tradition, however, sin entraps those bound by the law and those who know the law of God in their hearts.

Part 2: Romans 3:21—5 Paul teaches that the righteousness of God comes not from the law, but through faith in Jesus Christ. Whether or not one follows the Mosaic Law, it is faith that justifies a person. Paul speaks of justification for both the circumcised and the uncircumcised and God's intent to justify us by faith. Before the Mosaic Law, the righteousness of God came through the faith of Abraham. Thus the promise made to Abraham was not just for those who adhere to the Law, but for all who follow the example of Abraham, our father in faith. Therefore, we can boast of our afflictions that lead us to hope and love in Christ who laid down his life for us. Just as through the transgression of one, death came into the world, so through the righteous act of one (Christ), life came for all.

PART 1: GROUP STUDY (ROMANS 2—3:20)

Read aloud Romans 2—3:20.

2:1–11 God's Just Judgment

After his diatribe against those who do not allow themselves to believe, Paul seems to contradict his teaching. He seems to be judging sinners in his previous passage, and now he lashes out at those who judge others, telling them that they have no excuse for doing so. He claims that they actually condemn themselves because they perform the very deeds that they judge to be evil. Paul is actually telling them that they should not look complacently on his previous message and hold themselves excused while they judge others. Instead, they should test themselves against Paul's words. Paul does not perceive that he is judging others but that he is setting norms for judgment.

Although Paul does not name those who bear the name "Jew" as the targets of his words, he is actually addressing the Jews who believe that they, unlike the Gentiles, know the true God and the Mosaic Law. Later in this chapter, he will refer to those who call themselves Jews, but here he seems to be addressing the same people. The Jews would naturally agree with Paul's condemnation of idolatry, but Paul sees the rejection of Jesus Christ as a type of idolatry and so has a warning for his Jewish audience. The Jews will not only be accused of worshiping idols in the same manner as the pagans, but they will also be condemned for committing the sin of presuming that the goodness and patience of God will save them. Paul tells them that the kindness of God is an invitation to repentance.

Paul continues with his warning for his Jewish audience. He warns that just as the Jews of the past hardened their hearts against God (as in the Exodus), so now they are hardening their hearts against the gospel. When Moses led the people through the desert during the Exodus, the people became thirsty and rebelled against Moses, showing that they lacked trust in God. Their rebellion was considered a hardening of their hearts (Exodus 17:1–7). Paul tells the Jews of his own era that they must face God with their failings on the day of wrath, that is, the day of just judgment, when all will be understood clearly. On that day of judgment, all people, Jews as well as Gentiles, will receive a reward or punishment. Just as Paul acknowledged in the previous chapter of this letter that he was sent first to the Jews and then to the Gentiles, so he now states that the reward and punishment will be given out to all, first to the Jews and then to the Gentiles. Whether first or last, the Jews and the Gentiles who respond to God's loving justice will receive the same reward, while those who do not respond will receive the same punishment. Paul significantly states that God shows no partiality.

2:12–16 Judgment by the Interior Law

Paul teaches that God will judge all sinners within the framework of their knowledge of what is good or evil, and he contends that Jews and Gentiles alike have some knowledge of good and evil. Gentiles, who do not know the Mosaic Law, will be judged by their own interior call to live a good life, while the Jews, who have the Mosaic Law, will be judged according to that Law. Those who sin without knowing the Mosaic Law will perish without being judged by the Mosaic Law, and those who sin with knowledge of the Law will perish according to the demands of the Law. Possession of the Law by the Jews is not enough to be righteous in God's eyes, but those who obey the Law will be justified. When the Gentiles who do not know the Mosaic Law observe the Law in their hearts as they know it, they are living according to the prescriptions of the Law. Just as Paul declared earlier that one can know about God from a reflection on creation, so he now states that one can know the demands of the law written in a person's heart. Gentiles must follow the judgment of their conscience to tell them whether they are living in accordance with this inner law. On the day of judgment, their conscience will accuse or excuse them before God. On that day, judgment will come from God through Jesus Christ who knows the deep secrets of the heart.

2:17–29 Judgment by Mosaic Law

Although Paul has been addressing the Jews throughout this chapter, he names them as his audience for the first time in this passage. Confronting them, he uses the diatribe style found in his letter and addresses an imaginary audience without naming any individuals. He begins with the words, "Now if you call yourself a Jew and rely on the law and boast of God" (2:17). Here he is writing to the Jews who pride themselves on their knowledge of the Law and their call as the People of God, which is the foundation of their reason for boasting. They believe they have insight into God's will that others lack. Besides this supposed knowledge of God's will, they also believe they are able to make profound and correct judgments about the manner of living close to God. Because of their knowledge of the Law, they believe they can help the blind and become a light for those in darkness. Their knowledge of the Law leads them to believe they can teach the foolish and the simple.

After listing reasons for foolish pride and boasting, Paul confronts the Jews about their refusal to teach themselves. He asks those who teach others not to steal if they are stealing. For those who forbid adultery,

Paul asks if they are committing adultery. He asks if those who detest idols do not rob temples, implying that they are acting for their own gain. Although the Jews abhorred pagan temples, they were cautious about disgracing any of the temples. He challenges them as protectors of law to judge whether they are dishonoring the law of God by breaking it. Paul quotes from Isaiah (52:5) to show the Jews the evil they have done. In this quote, Isaiah tells the people how they have blasphemed God's name among the Gentiles by their actions.

Paul continues to challenge his audience by confronting those who believe they have fulfilled the Law by living out its rituals. Some of the Jews accepted circumcision without carrying out other demands of the Law, which makes Paul accuse them as living in the same manner as uncircumcised people. Jeremiah, an Old Testament prophet, urged the people to return to the Lord by circumcising their hearts as well as their bodies. He writes, "Be circumcised for the Lord, remove the foreskins of your hearts" (Jeremiah 4:4). In this passage Jeremiah taught that physical circumcision does not necessarily lead one to live as though he is dedicated to the Lord.

Paul returns to the importance of living out the spirit of the Law rather than the external precepts alone. He tells his listeners that the uncircumcised, who keep the inner law of their hearts, pass judgment on those circumcised Jews who do not live according to the Law. Following the insights of Jeremiah, Paul reminds his audience that true circumcision is not a mark found on the flesh but one that is found in the heart. It is not the letter of the law that matters.

When we read about Paul's attack on those who live according to the letter of the Law and not its spirit, we must be careful not to think that he is opposed to Jews. Paul cares deeply for his Jewish brothers and sisters, and he knows that many of them lived faithfully according to the precepts of the Mosaic Law. Because of his love for the Mosaic Law, Paul feels a need to lash out at those who have made a mockery of the Law. This passage ends by stating that it is the spirit, not the letter of the Law that is important. Others will not always favorably accept those who live this message. The Romans are told that they may not receive praise from any human source. In writing to the Romans, Paul is teaching that human praise is not important, but that one should rather seek praise from God.

3:1–8 Advantages of Being a Jew

Paul continues his imaginary debate by anticipating some objections to his statements about the Gentiles and Jews. After all he has said, one could infer that there was no advantage to being a Jew or to being circumcised. Paul, who was a good Jew himself and who cherished his Jewish roots, believed that God chose the people of Israel and the ancestors of Abraham as the foundation of God's promise to Israel. This was the case even though Paul himself preached about Christ and freedom from the Mosaic Law for Gentiles. When he was writing his letter to the Romans, Paul reached the point where he believed that the true descendants of Abraham were not those who followed him in the flesh (that is, not those bound to him by physical generation and circumcision), but those who followed the example and faith of Abraham.

In this passage of his Letter to the Romans, Paul begins to list the advantages of belonging to the Chosen People, but he names only the first advantage before becoming distracted by the example he uses. He states that the Jews received the great privilege of being entrusted with the Word of God, the Hebrew Scriptures. Paul digresses at this point and does not list any further advantages until he discusses them in a different context in Chapter 9 of this letter. Instead, he notes that God will not abandon God's covenant because of the unfaithfulness of some. Some Jews believed that a covenant existed only as long as both parties remained faithful to it, but the covenant made with God continues to exist because of God's faithfulness. Paul first asks if the covenant with God ceases because some Jews are unbelievers. Unlike many Jews, Paul does not accept the idea that a covenant ceases when one party breaks the covenant, and he adds that God will always be true to the covenant, no matter what others might do. Paul quotes from an Old Testament Psalm (116:11), which says that God will be proven true in the end, even if all people are liars.

Paul poses another question concerning the right of God to punish sinners. Some would contend that since a sinful person proves the justice of God by sinning, then God should not punish the sinful person. Without sin, we would never know of the justice of God. Paul answers that God's justice can only be shown in judgment. If we take judgment away from God, we can know nothing about God's justice. He notes that some might claim foolishly that the sinner actually points out the goodness of God and that sin can be a way of glorifying God. Some have apparently accused Paul of teaching this foolish message, and he strongly condemns them.

3:9–20 Universal Bondage of Sin

Paul questions whether the Jews have an advantage over others and then goes on to answer his own question by stating that the Jews are not better off, because Jews and Greeks alike are under the dominion of sin. For Paul and the people of his day, sin has a powerful grip on creation. Paul makes his point even more forceful by quoting from a series of Old Testament statements about the human condition. Besides the list of sins used in preaching in Paul's time, the preachers also used lists of quotations from the Hebrew Scriptures in order to emphasize a particular point. The list used here by Paul was most likely from one of these preset lists. In choosing this particular list of quotations from the Book of Psalms (14:1–3; 5:9; 140:3; 10:7; 36:1; and from Isaiah 59:7–8), Paul underlines the people's rejection of God. In short, the quotations tell us that no one is just and that all have gone in the wrong direction, unconcerned about a true search for God. Their mouths, like the tombs of the decaying dead, are the source of lies, curses, and bitterness. They run after evil and bloodshed and refuse to walk the path of peace. They lack a true fear of God. The image presented is of a person who completely lacks any form of righteousness. And the law applies to both Jews and Gentiles. The purpose of the Law is not to bring justification, but to enable a person to know what is sinful. The Jews who were familiar with the Scripture quotations used by Paul would have applied them to the Gentiles, but Paul applies them to all people.

Paul returns to the central theme of the letter by declaring that observance of the Law does not lead to justification. This can come only from God. The Law is simply a guide to help a person know what is sinful.

Review Questions

1. How would you apply Paul's warning about judging in the second chapter of Romans (2:1–11) to our own day?

2. In what way does the discussion about the law within our hearts in Romans (2:12–16) help us apply the message of Jesus to our life today?

3. How do you apply Paul's strong words on circumcision in Romans (2:17–29) to baptism?

4. Do you think that we need evil in the world to understand what is good? Explain.

Closing Prayer (SEE PAGE 20)

Pray the closing prayer now or after *lectio divina*.

Lectio Divina (SEE PAGE 11)

Relax your body and maintain a posture of prayer (back straight, eyes shut, feet flat on the floor). This exercise can take as long as you want, but in the context of this Bible study, 10 to 20 minutes should be sufficient.

The meditations that follow are provided only to help group participants use this prayer form, but note that *lectio* is intended to bring one to a place of prayerful contemplation where the Word of God speaks to the hearer from his or her heart. See page 11 for further instruction.

God's Just Judgment (2:1–11)

By warning the Jews against judging others, Paul is warning all people who consider themselves deserving of God's love. Some know the law and seem to be favored by God, but this neither frees them from practicing it nor does it give them the right to judge others. Whether knowledge of God's law comes through a revelation from God or through creation alone, everyone must act in a just manner before God. God shows no partiality. Whether people are first or last, the good will be rewarded and the evil will be condemned. Paul believes that God loves everyone equally.

✠ *What can I learn from this passage?*

Judgment by Interior Law (2:12–16)

For Paul, there is the law written in the Mosaic Law and the law within people that directs them to know good from evil. Christian law follows the command of Jesus that directs us to love the Lord our God with our whole person, and to love our neighbor as ourselves. Once we accept this law, all our actions are judged by it. Jesus quoted from the Old Testament in giving us this law, which means that the Mosaic Law already contained this call to total love of God and neighbor. Whether a person is a Jew who is bound by the Mosaic Law or is not a Jew and is bound by the law of Christ, all law boils down to love of God, neighbor, and a proper love of oneself. In accord with this law of love, Jews and Christians alike will be judged.

✠ *What can I learn from this passage?*

Judgment by the Mosaic Law (2:17–29)

Paul's message has an application to all people of faith. He warns the Jews that they must not only know and teach the Law, but they must live it in their hearts. We, too, know what God asks of us as taught through Jesus Christ. Therefore, Paul's warning falls on us as well. Knowing Jesus' law and externally living all the precepts and rituals of Christ's law is not enough. We must ask ourselves how Jesus' law permeates our whole existence, including our thinking, judging, forgiving, and acting. This is what Paul asks of the Jews, and he is indirectly asking the same of us. In Paul's Letter to the Romans, he offers a challenge to all who profess faith in Jesus and his message.

✠ *What can I learn from this passage?*

Advantages of Being a Jew (3:1–8)

Paul teaches that knowledge of God's law is a gift from God. Since it comes from God, it helps a person to know how to love God according to the Lord's designs. Paul draws his conclusions about God and covenant by basing them on his understanding of God's love. He teaches that God remains faithful to the covenant, even when others sin against it. He addresses those who say that God allows evil to help us understand goodness by noting the foolishness in this line of reasoning. He responds to this line of thinking by reminding then of God's love, explaining that God would never allow evil to exist just so people might recognize goodness. However, God's love shines on the good as well as those who are evil.

✠ *What can I learn from this passage?*

Universal Bondage of Sin (3:9–20)

Our aim in life is to love God. While it can be an advantage to have a law that identifies sinfulness, living by the letter of the law does not keep a person from sin. Viewed from this vantage point, it is the spirit of a person or the inner desire to live in harmony with God that aids a person to follow God's will. When we view the Law for the Jews and the inner law of creation for Gentiles from the angle of loving God, the judgment of God is important. God judges us with love, and we have the call to respond with love. This radical love always concerns the dedication of our heart, and not merely the external observance of the Law.

✠ *What can I learn from this passage?*

PART 2: INDIVIDUAL STUDY (ROMANS 3:21—5)

Day 1: Justification Apart From the Law (3:21–31)

In the previous passage, Paul noted the powerful grip of sin on the world, and he now offers a way to break this grip. He speaks of the "righteousness of God," which refers to an activity on the part of God whereby a right relationship is established between God and creation. Although the Law (Torah) and prophets have pointed to this righteousness, it does not depend on them. This righteousness of God, which sets all things right between God and creation, comes from faith in Jesus Christ. It is a gift freely given to all believers.

Because all people, Jews as well as Gentiles, are under the power of sinfulness, they are deprived of a share in the glory of God. Through faith in Jesus Christ, however, all share in the justice of God, not because they have earned it, but because God freely gives it to them. No one deserves or is owed this gift.

Through the ministry of Jesus Christ, redemption comes to all who are under the power of sin. This redemption does not imply that the sinner is bought back from someone, as though Satan owned the sinner. It implies that the sinner moves from one state (sinfulness) to another (freedom from the power of sin). This redemption is brought about by the shedding of Jesus' blood on the cross, and it expiates the sins of all believers. In this way, the justice of God becomes known to all, doing away with all sins committed in the past and patiently showing God's justice in the present.

Because justification is a gift from God that cannot be earned, no one has a right to boast about being justified. It comes not from any good works, but rather from faith in Jesus Christ. Because the Jews believe there is only one God, they must admit that it is the same God who justifies the Jews as well as the Gentiles. Paul declares that he does not mean to say that the Law should be done away with; rather he is saying that the Law fulfills its true purpose—the justice of God at work.

Lectio Divina

Spend 8 to 10 minutes in silent contemplation of the following passage:

The justice of God, which consists of a right relationship with God, overcomes the power of sin in the world. Jesus confronted sin and all its worldly power, and in his resurrection, he conquered the power of sin, as sin had no other weapon beyond death. Through the conquest of the power of sin, God established a harmony between God and creation. Since this is a gift that no one can earn through good works, it comes to us through the power of faith. Even when we perform our good deeds, God's response to those deeds is still a gift. We cannot claim that God owes us the gift, but we can recognize in faith that God freely gifts us with salvation.

✠ *What can I learn from this passage?*

Day 2: Abraham Justified by Faith (4:1–12)

Paul draws an example from the life of Abraham, the father of the Israelite nation. He declares that Abraham would have reason to boast if he could prove that his good deeds earned him his special blessing from God. Paul refers to a line in Genesis that states, "Abram put his faith in the LORD, who attributed it to him as an act of righteousness." (Genesis 15:6). Although Abraham himself did nothing to deserve this right relationship with God, God "credited" this justice to him because of his belief.

Paul develops his message by comparing the wages a worker deserves because of the work he has performed with the gift received by one who does nothing. When a person does nothing except believe in the one who establishes the right relationship with humans, then the gift this person receives must be credited strictly as justice and not as a just wage. Paul believes (as did the people of his own day) that David was the author of all the Psalms. To underline his message, Paul quotes from a psalm in which David commends the person of faith who is justified by God (32:1–2). Thus, God levies no guilt on a person whose sins are "covered."

Paul continues his argument by asserting that Abraham was justified before his circumcision, that is, before he began to follow the Law.

It was almost thirty years after this call by God that Abraham received his circumcision. Paul sees circumcision as a sign of justification already received, rather than as a cause of justification. Because he was justified before his circumcision, Paul declares that Abraham proves that justification comes through faith. Abraham was the father of the uncircumcised as well as the circumcised and the one who gave a living example to all.

Lectio Divina

Spend 8 to 10 minutes in silent contemplation of the following passage:

Abraham's early commitment to God followed no external commands that he had to follow. Abraham existed before the Mosaic Law. But it was his faith that led God to reward him. Since Abraham lived by faith and not by the Law, his life showed the justification and love of God. It was God who acted on Abraham, not Abraham who performed acts in accord with the Law in order to please God. God is as active in our life as God was in the life of Abraham. God's justification of our lives does not depend on our actions alone, but on the living faith that guides our actions. True faith will always lead us to act with love toward God, and God will always respond with love.

✠ *What can I learn from this passage?*

Day 3: Inheritance Through Faith (4:13–25)

Paul emphasizes the point that the promise made to Abraham and passed on to his descendants—the promise that they would inherit the world—did not depend upon the Law. If this were so, then there would be no meaning to faith, or to the promise, because the promise would then depend on the activities of human beings. Because God's promise is based on faith, it includes all people, as the Scriptures proclaim (Genesis 22:17–18,15:5).

Abraham believed that God gave life to the dead and birth to those not yet born. Paul tells us of the unflinching faith of Abraham, who believed in God and became the father of many nations. Paul conveniently omits

Abraham's laughter and hesitation at the news that he was to be the father of a child in his old age (Genesis 17:17). The dead to whom God gives life refers to the aged bodies of Abraham and of Sarah. Because God controls death and birth, God is able to bring to life the reproductive abilities of Abraham and Sarah, thus producing a new life. Paul repeats his message for the sake of emphasis. It was because of the faith of Abraham that he was justified.

Just as Abraham's faith led him to believe that God could bring a child forth from an aged man and a barren woman, so the faith of Christians leads them to believe that God raised Jesus from the dead. Christians, by believing that Jesus died for their sins and was raised for their justification, share in this true relationship, which is called the justice of God.

Lectio Divina

Spend 8 to 10 minutes in silent contemplation of the following passage:

> Abraham's faith led to the promise God made to him and his descendants. The same faith that led Abraham to believe that God could bring life to a barren womb leads Christians to believe that God raised Jesus from the dead. Christians believe in the possibility of a right and harmonious relationship with God resulting from the death and resurrection of Jesus. The faith of each Christian flourishes as a result of the love God has shown in Jesus' resurrection, a faith that is not merited but given freely by God.

> ☩ *What can I learn from this passage?*

Day 4: Life in God (5:1–11)

Because of justification by faith, Paul declares that we are now at peace with God through Jesus Christ, our Lord. To the Hebrews, the word peace included a number of gifts, including contentment, harmony with God, and joy. Through Jesus Christ, the believer now stands before God with a new relationship (grace).

Paul here finds three reasons for boasting. The idea of such boasting is not to brag about oneself, but to expound on the wonders that come from the goodness of God. His first boast looks to the hope we all have in sharing in the glory of God. His second boast, strangely enough, looks toward the suffering we must endure. The boasting is not done to express a sadistic approach to life, but instead to look beyond the suffering to the results that come from enduring it patiently. Through the virtue that comes from patiently enduring suffering, the Christian has reason to hope. Because God's love has already come to us through the Holy Spirit, such hope will not leave us disappointed. Again this love that comes from God is not earned, but freely given.

While we were still under the power of sin, Christ died for us. Paul recognizes the difficulty in dying, even if it be for a friend. That Jesus would die for us while we were still sinners proves the depth of his love for us. If Jesus died for us when we were such terrible sinners, how much more will he save us now that we have been reconciled with God through his death? Paul boasts this third time with the assurance of boasting not in his own name, but in the name of Jesus Christ. He boasts about God with whom we have all been reconciled.

Lectio Divina

Spend 8 to 10 minutes in silent contemplation of the following passage:

Paul changes the idea of boasting. He boasts, not because of something he had done, but because of what God has done. Christ brings us peace, which is contentment, harmony with God, and joy in the Lord. First, Paul boasts about the wonders of God's blessings bestowed on us. His second boast is about God's great love, which led Christ to suffer for us. The Christian can look beyond the suffering of Christ and realize the outstanding love of Christ who died. In turn, this fills us with hope and leads us to the virtue of enduring suffering. The third reason for boasting is that Christ has reconciled us with God. Paul realizes the foolishness of boasting about a holiness that neglects the reality that God's love for us is the real reason for boasting.

✠ *What can I learn from this passage?*

Day 5: Grace and Life through Christ (5:12–21)

In this passage, Paul contrasts the results of Adam's sin with the gift that comes from Jesus Christ. Through one person's sin, many died. Death in this sense refers to spiritual death in sin. Because all people sinned, all fell under the power of this spiritual death. Although the law that helped a person identify sin did not yet exist, sin did exist in the world. Paul tells us that this sin of the people was not in violation of a precept, such as that committed by Adam, but sin still prevailed.

Paul contrasts the gift that came through Jesus Christ with the effects of the sin committed through the one man, Adam. The gift of Jesus far surpassed the offense of Adam. Condemnation followed the single offense of Adam, whereas justification through Christ came after many offenses. Whereas death resulted from the sin of Adam, the far greater gift of justification came through the one man, Jesus Christ. In summary, Paul contrasts the condemnation that comes through the disobedience of Adam with the justification that comes through the obedience of Jesus Christ.

Paul tells us that the Law increased sin because people were able to identify their sinful actions as a result of knowing the Law. On the other hand, those who can clearly identify sin are more capable of understanding the extent of God's gift given through Jesus Christ. Where sin abounded, the grace that came through Jesus Christ far surpassed it.

Lectio Divina

Spend 8 to 10 minutes in silent contemplation of the following passage:

> Paul helps us understand the extent of God's love for us by contrasting the sin of the first human being with the love of God that brought us justification through the suffering, death, and resurrection of Jesus. Justification leads to a loving harmony with God, but this was gained at a great price. Knowledge of what is sinful can lead us to recognize sin in the world, but it also enables us to understand God's great love involved in freeing us from sin. Harmony with God is freely given from the Lord. Once we

realize this, we have the call to respond to such love by avoiding sin at all costs.

✠ *What can I learn from this passage?*

Review Questions

1. Why do Catholics refuse to believe that faith alone is all we need for salvation, regardless of what works we perform, whether good or evil?

2. How does Paul consider each of us to be an offspring of Abraham?

3. In what way does our sinfulness prove how much God loves us?

4. What does Paul mean when he says in Romans that "through the obedience of one the many will be made righteous" (5:19)? Discuss.

Justification and Christian Life

ROMANS 6—8

I consider that the sufferings of this present time are as nothing compared with the glory to be revealed for us (8:18).

Opening Prayer (SEE PAGE 20)

Context

Part 1: Romans 6—7:12 Paul declares that through our baptism, we have died with Christ and have been raised to new life, just as Jesus suffered and died and was raised on the third day. We no longer live for ourselves, but for Christ. Death no longer has power over Jesus, but we must still be prepared to overcome temptation in our efforts to live for Christ. A person can choose to be a slave to sin or to live in obedience to God. Paul speaks of the Law as something good, but it can allure a person to sin by naming what is sinful.

Part 2: Romans 7:13—8 Paul questions himself, asking why he does those things he considers evil. The Spirit desires what is right, but the sinful flesh takes control of him. He asks who will deliver him from this evil flesh, and the answer is that God delivers us through Jesus Christ. What the law could not do, the power of the Son of God did. The Spirit of God who raised Jesus from the dead is alive in us. Those who are led by the Spirit are children of God. All of creation is struggling with evil, but the Spirit helps us in our weakness. For those who love God, all things work together for good. Nothing is able to deter them from serving God.

PART 1: GROUP STUDY (ROMANS 6—7:12)

Read aloud Romans 6—7:12.

6:1-14 Raised in Christ

Paul turns his attention to a question he answered for the Jews earlier in his letter, namely, the motive to sin in order to manifest the abundance of God's gifts (Romans 3:8). In this passage, Paul directly and explicitly tells Christians that he rejects this manner of thinking. It is foolish to think that one who dies to sin can live in it. He clarifies his message by making his readers aware of what happens at baptism, alluding to the baptismal practice of his time. That is, the person to be baptized would go down into the water, be completely submerged, and come out to live a new life as a Christian. Paul expresses this as a "death" (going down into the water) and a "resurrection" (coming out of the water). Through baptism, one is buried with Christ and just as Christ was raised from the dead to a new life by the glory of the Father, so also the baptized share in this newness of life in Christ.

Through death and resurrection, a person is united with Christ. By uniting with the death of Jesus, one also shares in the resurrection of Christ. When Paul speaks of this union with Christ, he means that a person has grown together with him, achieving a true sharing in Christ's life. This is the only place in the New Testament where this notion is mentioned. Paul tells his readers that a person's turning from sin should be as dramatic as the crucifixion, which tore Jesus from this life and led him to a new life of glory. The power of sin that made slaves of God's creatures has lost its grip. Through this death in Christ, the person (the sinful body) has been freed from this slavery to sin.

The Christian belief expressed by Paul is that a person who has died with Christ (through baptism) shall also live with him. Once Jesus has died, he cannot die any more, and once he has been raised, he lives for God. Death no longer has any power over him. As followers of Jesus, Christians must consider themselves dead to the power of sin and alive for God in Christ Jesus.

Although Christians have died to sin and risen to a new life in Christ, this does not mean they are free from all temptations and allurements of the world. Thus, Paul urges his Christian readers to give themselves to God as instruments of righteousness rather than allow themselves to become slaves to sin and instruments of sin against God. In this way, all can live anew as a people raised to new life in Christ Jesus. Though the struggle with sin will continue, it has lost its power over those who live in God's grace.

6:15–23 Freed From Sin

Paul draws a conclusion from all he has said in the opening passage of this chapter. A person may choose to become a slave of sin, which leads to spiritual death, or a slave of obedience to God, which leads to righteousness. One cannot choose both sin and justification. Paul adds a gentle apology for using the image of slavery with his Roman audience, but he uses the term "slavery" because it speaks more clearly of their weak human nature.

As he continues to use the image of slavery, Paul urges his readers, once slaves to sin, to give themselves as slaves of righteousness, leading them to sanctification. Paul reminds his readers how they were not slaves to righteousness when *they* were slaves of sin, and they received the wages of sin, which lead to spiritual death. Paul sees the outcome of sin as a payment, or wage, for the manner of life chosen. Those who are slaves to God, however, do not receive a wage; instead they receive a free gift from God, which leads to holiness and eternal life in union with Christ Jesus, the Lord.

7:1–6 Freedom From the Law

Paul now directs his attention to freedom from the Mosaic Law, although some commentators believe that Paul is speaking about all law. He explains that Law binds only those who are living, having jurisdiction as long as a person is alive. Using the example of marriage, Paul applies this example to Christians. For he explains that a woman is no longer bound by the law of marriage when her husband dies, and she is free to marry without committing the sin of adultery. The dead husband is the Law, and the new husband is Christ, who was raised from the dead so that Christians might bear fruit for God. While a person lived by the Law, the Law was able to arouse that person's evil passions, which led to spiritual death. Now, having died to this Law through Christ, Christians serve with a new spirit, no longer enslaved to the Law.

7:7–12 Sin Present Before the Law

Paul's words seem to imply that the Law that comes from God is actually the same as sin. Thus, Paul denies the claim that he teaches that sin and the Law are the same. Sin was present before the Law, but once the Law came, sin took the opportunity to use the Law to entice people to evil. Here, Paul is speaking of sin as if it were able to act. Many commentators believe that Paul is referring to the temptation and sin of Adam. Adam committed his sin because of the precept that tempted him to that sin.

In this passage, Paul uses the word "I" not to refer to himself alone, but so that the reader would refer to himself or herself while reading. Paul actually refers to all people. When Paul says "I" sinned and died, he is speaking for all. The Law that comes from God is good, holy, and just, but instead of becoming a Law that led to life, it became for some a Law that made sin enticing and led to spiritual death. According to Paul, the Law was not the cause of his spiritual death, but rather his own sin. The misuse of this good and holy Law was its root cause prior to his conversion. Paul is therefore indicating that knowing what is sinful can entice a person to sin; and the Law provides this knowledge of sin.

Review Questions

1. How does the death and resurrection of Christ affect our lives?

2. What does Paul warn early Christians about regarding sin and grace? Explain.

3. Does Paul believe that people of faith need laws to help identify what is sinful? Discuss.

Closing Prayer (SEE PAGE 20)

Pray the closing prayer now or after *lectio divina*.

Lectio Divina (SEE PAGE 11)

Relax your body and maintain a posture of prayer (back straight, eyes shut, feet flat on the floor). This exercise can take as long as you want, but in the context of this Bible study, 10 to 20 minutes should be sufficient.

The meditations that follow are provided only to help group participants use this prayer form, but note that *lectio* is intended to bring one to a place of prayerful contemplation where the Word of God speaks to the hearer from his or her heart. See page 11 for further instruction.

Raised in Christ (6:1–14)

Through our baptism, we die to sin and are born in Christ Jesus. This is one of the great mysteries of our Christian lives. A woman once read about the life of Mother Teresa, how she was able to hug and show affection to the poorest and dirtiest of homeless people. After witnessing Mother Teresa's story, the woman told a friend that her life changed in an instant. She knew Paul's words that said as followers of Christ, we are dead to sin and alive in Christ; however she never gave much credence to the words until she read about Mother Teresa.

Though the woman had no plans to leave her neighborhood and travel to areas where she could care for people as Mother Teresa did, she knew that she could reflect Christ by adjusting her manner of life in simple ways. Therefore, she vowed to try to become more aware that she no longer lived for herself alone, but for Christ. At the point of her conversion, the woman decided to meditate each day on the idea of dying to sin and rising with Christ.

✠ *What can I learn from this passage?*

Freed From Sin (6:15–23)

Jesus said, "Where your treasure is, there also will your heart be" (Matthew 6:21). Paul uses the image of slavery and freedom, implying that we become slaves of whatever we choose in life. If we choose evil, then we are slaves to evil. If we choose Christ and goodness, then we are slaves to goodness and love of the Lord. What enslaves us? Do we know what our heart truly yearns to receive? Ironically, those who are slaves to sin receive the *wages of sin*, or in other words, a spiritual death often accompanied with unhappiness; but those who choose to be slaves of God are promised eternity in union with Jesus Christ, the true desire of our hearts. Choosing to live in union with Jesus allows us to receive the gift promised us by Christ, a gift freely given by God to the beloved.

✠ *What can I learn from this passage?*

Freedom From the Law (7:1–6)

A businessman became very successful and rich through his investments and wanted to share his gifts with his elderly parents by purchasing a one- floor new house for them. They lived in an old house that was literally "falling apart." To the businessman's surprise, his parents refused the new house, saying that they spent sixty years together in their home and though it was old and in need of repair, they still wanted to remain in the old house. When people have lived for a long time with a particular way of acting or believing, it is difficult for them to change.

Paul was attempting to teach new ideas to the Jews and Gentiles in Rome. He taught them that they are baptized into Christ, meaning that they are baptized into the Lord's death and resurrection. Just as a person in a marriage whose spouse has died has the right to accept another as a spouse, Paul tries to convince his readers that they can accept this new law that consists in living for Christ. They are invited by Paul to die to sin and rise in Christ, centering all they do on Jesus. In our world today, the idea of dying to sin or our old ways of acting and living in Christ is challenging, but in freedom we are invited to order our lives in such a way that sets us apart from the world—an ordered and holy way of life.

✠ *What can I learn from this passage?*

Sin Present Before the Law (7:7–12)

Adam and Eve are forbidden to eat the enticing fruit of the tree of good and evil that stands in the middle of the garden, a place they pass by every day. Christians commonly call the fruit of the tree "the forbidden fruit." Once Adam and Eve were told not to eat of the fruit of the tree, the fruit becomes even more enticing. Paul implies that the law has this very same effect. Once we are told not to act this or that way, we can sometimes find the "forbidden fruit" more enticing. Though he is not saying that the law is bad, Paul does stress that the law emphasizes the allurements of those things it prohibits. Still, the law of Christ is a law of love—God, neighbor, and self. Thus, it points us in the direction of good actions. Every day we pass by trees of good and evil that stand precisely on the paths we trod. But if we keep our focus on Christ, we will always be moving beyond the forbidden fruit to Christ.

✠ *What can I learn from this passage?*

PART 2: INDIVIDUAL STUDY (ROMANS 7:13—8)

Day 1: Struggles Between Good and Evil (7:13–25)

Paul uses a typical Jewish image of his day when he speaks about the war waged within himself between the flesh and the spirit. We must not confuse this with our imagery of body and soul. Paul considers the flesh to be one's attachment to worldly goods; he considers the spirit to be one's attachment to the things of God. The flesh leads to sin and the spirit leads to grace.

Therefore, when Paul speaks of himself in this passage, he again is most likely speaking on behalf of all people. He recognizes his own internal battle and wishes to follow the spiritual law, but the power of the flesh causes him to act against his own spiritual will. In Paul, the power of the flesh overcomes the power of the spirit, and he finds himself at the mercy of the law of sin rather than the law of God. In desperation, Paul cries out for some outside help and wonders who can free him from this power of death.

The answer comes to Paul, who expresses a prayer of praise to God through Jesus Christ. Paul recognizes that this help will come from Jesus Christ. So he ends this passage by repeating his problem: his mind serves the law of God, but his flesh serves the law of sin.

Lectio Divina

Spend 8 to 10 minutes in silent contemplation of the following passage:

In the Gospel of Matthew, we read that one night Jesus came walking on water to his disciples in the midst of a storm. When Peter recognizes Jesus, he asks Christ to allow him to walk on the water. Jesus agrees and Peter thus gets out of the boat and begins to walk, but he suddenly looks around at the storm and starts to sink. In a panic, he looks back to Christ and cries out, "Lord, save me." Jesus catches him and chides him for his lack of faith (see Matthew 14:22–31).

Paul, as holy and dedicated as he is, shares the same struggle faced by Peter and all of us. He knows that he wishes to follow the law of Christ in an effort to prove his love for God, but he realizes that the enticing storms of this world, which he refers to as allurements of the flesh, overcome the spirit of the Lord within him and so he finds himself immersed in the law of sin rather than the law of love. Like us, he recognizes his weakness in the face of these worldly allurements, and he cries out for help. And with us, Paul confidently praises Christ as his only help and hope.

✠ *What can I learn from this passage?*

Day 2: The Flesh and the Spirit (8:1–17)

In the previous passage, Paul used the word *law* in two different ways. The Mosaic Law refers to the precepts given by God, while the law of the flesh refers to the magnetic pull of one's life toward sin. Paul states that those who live in Jesus Christ face no condemnation, because they live according to the law of the Spirit of life in Jesus Christ. This law refers to the influence of the Spirit on those who give themselves to Christ, and frees a person from the power (law) of sin and death. The Mosaic Law, in contrast, has no power, because it cannot control the fact that the flesh is prone toward sin.

Paul praises God through Jesus Christ in the previous passage to reveal the mystery of Jesus coming in the form of sinful flesh. Although Jesus was not sinful himself, he came as a sin offering to conquer the power of sin. Those who choose to follow the way of the flesh commit themselves to spiritual death and enmity with God, while those who choose to follow the way of the Spirit commit themselves to spiritual life and peace. In this passage, Paul continually refers to the work of the Spirit.

He tells the Romans that they do not belong to the flesh because they have the Spirit of God dwelling in them. Through their baptism, they belong to Christ. The presence of Christ in them means they are dead to sin and alive in the Spirit. The Spirit dwelling in Christians will raise their bodies to new life just as this same Spirit raised Jesus from the dead.

Although Paul tells us that we are people in debt—but not in debt to the flesh—though he never tells us to whom we are in debt. He declares that those who live according to the flesh will die, and those who put sinful deeds to death by the power of the Spirit will live. Then he continues to speak of the gifts that belong to those who are led by the Spirit of God. Through this gift of the Spirit of God, Christians do not become slaves but share an adoption that actually makes them sons and daughters of God. Through this adoption, an inner change takes place that enables the children of God to call out in a confident and intimate manner to God, who is "Abba." We are not slaves, but actually heirs of God with Christ. This is a gift freely given by God. Through this gift, we are called to share in every aspect of Christ's life, including his suffering, that leads to glorification. The word *Abba* gets lost in our formal English translation. The closest translation we can come to in English is the word *daddy,* but most translations use the more formal term, *father.*

Lectio Divina

Spend 8 to 10 minutes in silent contemplation of the following passage:

Jesus took upon himself a human nature like ours to confront the power of sin in the world, giving us a choice of whether to follow the way of the flesh or that of the Spirit. Although Jesus conquered the power of the flesh in the world, we still live in the flesh, meaning we live with an enticement to sin. Through Jesus, God invites us to live in the Spirit, which brings us into union with the resurrected Christ. And by baptism into Christ, we are raised to a new life as adopted children of God and heirs of God in union with Christ. Therefore, we enter into union with every aspect of Christ's life, which includes his suffering, death, and resurrection. By living every aspect of our life in union with Christ, we link our suffering with the suffering of Christ, and we share as well in his glorification.

✠ *What can I learn from this passage?*

Day 3: Destiny to Glory (8:18–30)

Despite the sufferings of the present, Paul looks with hope to future glory. He pictures all of creation straining for the day when all will be revealed, following a common biblical view that perceives all of creation in need of salvation. The power of sin in the world made the world subject to frustration, but God offers hope for fulfillment in Christ. Thus, the world shares in this glorious freedom as we become heirs and children of God.

In the same manner in which a woman undergoes labor pains, so all of creation (not just the human family) groans in agony until the day of fulfillment. Even Christians who already have the first fruits, that is, the gift of the Spirit, must wait for complete fulfillment at the end of time. Hope is a virtue that seeks those things that are not seen. If something is seen, we cannot identify our longing as true hope; but hope leads to endurance.

Because of our weakness, we need the gift of the Spirit to teach us how to pray. The Spirit enters creation to such a degree that our groaning and sighs become those of the Spirit. And it is the will of God that the Spirit prays on behalf of all those who place their trust in the Lord.

Lectio Divina

Spend 8 to 10 minutes in silent contemplation of the following passage:

A teacher held up a piece of paper with a dot on it and asked the students what they saw. All of them said that they saw the dot. The teacher then proceeded to ask them why no one said that they saw a paper that was all white except for the dot in the center. The object of the lesson was to point out that we see the dark spots of creation, but miss the white surrounding these spots. People tend to worry about all the evil in the world, but there are many more good people than evil people. Unfortunately, the good people do not always get spotlighted in our headlines.

Paul knows there is suffering and evil in the world, but he also knows that the Holy Spirit helps us in our weakness and frustration. Because of the Holy Spirit, we can have hope that God's creation is still good and is moving toward a fulfillment in God. The many good people in God's creation must hope because the Spirit "intercedes for the holy ones according to God's will" (Romans 8:27).

✠ *What can I learn from this passage?*

Day 4: God's Overwhelming Love in Christ (8:29–39)

All believers know that God makes everything work together for good. God foresaw those who would believe in God's message and predestined them to share in the gifts of Jesus Christ. When Paul speaks of predestination, he is not referring to individual predestination, as though God already determined who would be saved, but as a reference to those who love God. By God's plan, those who love God are predestined to a state of justification and glory, for God predestined those who love God to be called, justified, and glorified.

Paul asks several rhetorical questions in this passage, all of which receive an answer. Through his questions, Paul uses the term "we" and "us" as referring to all believers. He teaches that God, who allowed Jesus to be led off to death, will certainly grant us many more gifts. The God who justifies will certainly not accuse the weak. Jesus Christ, who died, was raised up, sits in glory at the right hand of God, and who continually intercedes for us, will not condemn us. The basic message of these lines is, "If God is for us, who can be against us" (Romans 8:31).

Paul next asks who will separate Christians from the love of Christ. The answer is that nothing inside or outside of creation has the power to separate the Christian from Christ. Throughout all human hardship, Christians are always able to conquer because of God's love. Paul makes a reference to Psalm 44:23, which speaks of the followers of Jesus as being slain all day, and like sheep being led to the slaughter; but he implies that nothing can deter Christians from the love of God. Among the heavenly powers, no one in present or past history, no one in the highest heavens, no one in the depths of the earth, no one at all will be able to separate Christians from this love of God that comes through Jesus Christ, who is Lord.

Lectio Divina

Spend 8 to 10 minutes in silent contemplation of the following passage:

Although many of the martyrs, who did not seek death, faced death with faith and courage, their example led others to believe in Christ. Even death itself could not deter the martyrs from professing faith in Jesus. Paul teaches an overwhelming trust in God's love and protection in our lives. Referring to the good deeds performed by Christ, Paul notes that God who allowed Jesus to die for us will shower us with gifts. The Lord will not accuse us in moments of weakness, or condemn us, but will always offer us strength when we need it. We can make Paul's faith our faith by living a life in which nothing can separate us from the love of God, whether in heaven, on earth, or in the depths of the earth. Paul's total dedication to Christ offers us a model of trust and endurance of one living in union with Christ Jesus, the Lord.

✠ *What can I learn from this passage?*

Review Questions

1. How does our own inclination to sin compare with that of Paul as found in Romans (7:13–25)?

2. What is meant by living by the spirit and not by the flesh in the passages in this individual study?

3. Do you value being called a child of God? Explain.

4. Does Paul's message about creation groaning in pain as found in Romans (8:18–27) help us to understand our need for the Spirit in our lives? If so, explain why.

5. What does Paul mean when he speaks about predestination in Romans (8:28–39)?

Jews and Gentiles
in God's Plan

ROMANS 9—11

---

*But how can they call on him in whom they have not believed?
And how can they believe in him of whom they have not heard?
And how can they hear without someone to preach? And how
can people preach unless they are sent (10:14–15).*

Opening Prayer (SEE PAGE 20)

Context

Part 1: Romans 9—10 For many Jewish Christians, Paul may
sound like he is rejecting his Jewish heritage, but he expresses
his great love for the Jewish people to show that his intent is not
to reject his Jewish roots. He teaches, however, that not all who
claim ancestry from Abraham in the flesh are true Israelites. God
has not rejected them, but they have rejected God. Just as God
chose Isaac over his elder brother Ishmael, and chose Jacob over
his elder brother Esau, so God can choose spiritual ancestry as
God wishes. Only those who call upon God with faith are truly
following God's law. Among the Jews there is a remnant chosen
by grace to live by faith and not by works of the Law alone. The
reason many of the Jews did not come to righteousness is that
they followed the Law without faith, whereas many of the Gentiles
lived by faith.

Part 2: Romans 11 Paul questions whether God has rejected the Chosen People. He answers that God has preserved a remnant, just as God preserved a remnant during the time of Elijah the prophet. Through the faults of the Israelites, the Gentiles have flourished. As the apostle to the Gentiles, Paul can rejoice in the faith of the Gentiles, but even Gentiles must beware lest they suffer the same fate as the Israelites who persecuted Jesus. Just as the mercy of God used the Israelites to bring the Gentiles to faith, now God can use the Gentiles to bring the Israelites to faith.

PART 1: GROUP STUDY (ROMANS 9—10)

Read aloud Romans 9—10.

9:1–5 Paul's Love for Israel

Some believed that Paul was rejecting his own Jewish heritage in his preaching to the Gentiles, but Paul defends himself and explains the importance he places on his Jewish roots. He declares that he continually speaks the truth, but he is forced to experience constant pain and sorrow because many Jews reject his message about Jesus. To stress his point, he exaggerates by telling his readers that he is willing to separate himself from Christ for the sake of his brothers and relatives. And Paul informed his readers in the previous passage that nothing could separate him from Christ.

Therefore, Paul praises God for the gifts bestowed upon the Jewish people. The Israelites were the chosen, adopted children of God, who were guided by the glory of God's presence throughout history. They could claim a covenant with God, a Law (Torah), the Temple worship, and the promise. They shared in the special gifts given to the patriarchs, Abraham, Isaac, and Jacob, and they shared in the privilege of having the Messiah come from their ancestry. These gifts are reason enough to praise God.

9:6–24 God's Free Choice

This passage may sound as though God has already chosen those who will be saved and those who will not, but Paul intends it as a warning for those Israelites who believe that it is through physical descent as a child of Abraham that they are true descendants of Abraham. He rejects this idea, saying that true descent does not depend on the flesh but on God's plan. Some may feel that God's word has failed, but Paul's message is that it has not failed. But Jews and Gentiles must understand God's freedom in choosing true descendants of Abraham. To prove God's freedom, Paul draws an example from the life of Abraham and his offspring.

Abraham had a wife named Sarah who reached old age without having a child. Sarah, following the custom of her day, gave Hagar, her slave girl, to Abraham so that he may bear a child by Hagar. In Abraham's era, the child of a slave girl would be seen as a child of the one who owned her. Hagar gave birth to Ishmael, which makes Ishmael Abraham's first-born child, which would entitle him the right to inherit the blessings promised to Abraham. God promises Sarah that she would bear a son in her old age, and this promise was indeed fulfilled when she bore a son named Isaac. Although Isaac was the second son born to Abraham and ordinarily would not be considered the true heir, God chose Isaac over his older brother Ishmael.

Lest some think that Paul's example of Ishmael and Isaac is not a good one since they had different mothers, he uses the sons of Isaac—Jacob and Esau—to further demonstrate his point. They both had the same mother, Rebekah. Esau and Jacob were twins, and Esau was born first, but God chose Jacob, the second one born, as an heir to the promise. God said that it would be through Isaac that Abraham's offspring would be the children of promise, and God chose Jacob, the second son of Isaac, as the one to continue as an heir to the promise given to Abraham and his descendants. Jacob was chosen before he doing anything to deserve his role of an heir to the promise. This shows that God chooses freely and not because of some particular work a person has performed.

Paul quotes from the Book of Malachi (1:3) when he tells of God's love for Jacob and God's hatred for Esau. Lest we believe that God actually hated Esau, we should remember that the Scriptures often use complete opposites to emphasize a point. In wishing to show God's love for Jacob, the Scriptures exaggerate God's rejection of Esau. The term "hate" in Semitic mentality means "loves less."

Paul declares that God's action should not be considered to be unjust. In the Book of Exodus (33:19), God's mercy and pity are given as God chooses. These are gifts that come from God, not gifts earned by humans. Although the Book of Exodus describes Pharaoh ignoring Moses by his own free choice (7:14–22), Paul presents his stubbornness as an act of God. Through Pharaoh's rejection of Moses' request, the power of God over the Egyptian army was able to be manifest. According to Paul's argument, God bestows mercy on some and causes others to harden their hearts.

Paul carries on his debate by posing an obvious question concerning the right of God to find fault with a person who seems to have no choice but to follow the will of God. Paul does not answer the objection, but he does make an issue of the boldness needed to question God. He uses the image of a potter working with clay, an image often used in the Scriptures (Isaiah 29:16, 45:9; Jeremiah 18:6). A potter can make some vessels for a special use, and other vessels for ordinary use. In the same way, God can make vessels for showing the wrath of God as well as those used to glorify God. God's chosen vessels come from among the Gentiles as well as from among the Jews.

9:25–33 Witness of the Prophets

Paul adapts a quotation from Hosea (2:23) to show how God calls the Gentiles to also be the People of God. Hosea spoke of Israelites who rejected their role as God's people and were taken back by God. So Paul adjusts this quotation and applied it to the Gentiles. Quoting from Isaiah (10:22ff; 1:9), he reminds his readers that the prophet foresaw the day when only a remnant of Israel would carry on its hope. If this did not happen, the Israelites would disappear from the earth like the inhabitants of the cities of Sodom and Gomorrah, which were completely destroyed by God.

Paul continues to answer his own questions by stating that the Gentiles, although not seeking justification, came to find it because of their faith. The Israelites, on the other hand, sought justification by practicing the Law, but did not receive it. Paul places two quotations from Isaiah side by side to underline his message. Isaiah speaks of the stone of Zion (28:16) that will become the stumbling stone (8:14). The stumbling stone is the belief that justification comes from works, but actually comes through faith.

10:1–13 Faith in Christ

Paul continues to show his concern for the Israelites as he prays for their salvation. He recognizes their zeal for God but points out that their zeal is misguided, since it places its trust in the Law rather than in the righteousness of God. The Israelites still believed in the Law, but with the coming of Christ, the Law came to an end. Justification comes into the world through Christ, not through the Law. So Paul applies a series of Old Testament texts to Christ, quoting from the Book of Deuteronomy to show that the rewards of the Law come from the Law, and that righteousness comes from faith. He asks his audience to wonder who will go to heaven to bring Christ down; or who will go down into the place of the dead to bring Christ back? But, Christ has already come from heaven in his human form, and has been raised from the dead by God.

Paul adapts a quotation from Deuteronomy (30:14) to express (2:32) that the word of faith he preaches is on the lips and in the heart of those who believe. Those who profess faith in Jesus as the Lord (from heaven) and as the one raised up (from the dead) will be saved. The heart (faith) leads to righteousness and the lips (profession of faith) to salvation. Paul quotes from the prophet Joel to stress that anyone who has faith in Jesus Christ will be saved (2:32). The original quotation from Joel refers to God, but here Paul applies it to Christ.

Because there is one Lord, the Jew as well as the Gentile shares in this faith. All who call on the name of the Lord will be saved.

10:14–21 Faith Comes Through Hearing

Through a series of questions followed by a series of Scripture quotations, Paul reveals that the Israelites have no excuse for not believing in Jesus. Through these questions, Paul actually states that a person cannot call on Jesus unless he or she has heard about him and believes in him. In order to do this, a preacher must be chosen and sent to them to preach this Word. After he poses his questions, Paul answers each one. Quoting from Isaiah (52:7), Paul tells his listeners that Scripture says preachers will be sent, and considers himself one of these preachers who brought the Word to the Israelites.

Despite this preaching, the Israelites rejected the message. This is not unexpected, as Isaiah had predicted this rejection (53:1). Paul emphatically states that the Israelites have indeed heard the Word about Jesus Christ. He again calls on the Scriptures to support his statement, quoting from Psalm 19:4, which to Paul supports the belief that the preaching about Jesus reaches to the ends of the earth. He then quotes Moses (Deuteronomy 32:21) to support his statement that all people of many different nations will hear the Word. Here Paul is referring to the Gentiles. He completes his message about their acceptance of the Word about Jesus by quoting the prophet Isaiah (65:1ff), who has the Lord proclaiming that those who did not seek him accepted the message. Lest anyone feel that the Lord has abandoned Israel for the Gentiles, Paul wishes to show that it is Israel who has abandoned the Lord. To do this, he quotes again from Isaiah (65:2), who tells of the Lord continually reaching out to the people (Israel) who stubbornly refused to believe.

Review Questions

1. Would you say that the Israelites are still the chosen people today?
2. How does God's free choice as described in Romans (9:6–33) affect our lives today?
3. In what way are we sent to share the Word of God?

Closing Prayer (SEE PAGE 20)

Pray the closing prayer now or after *lectio divina*.

Lectio Divina (SEE PAGE 11)

Relax your body and maintain a posture of prayer (back straight, eyes shut, feet flat on the floor). This exercise can take as long as you want, but in the context of this Bible study, 10 to 20 minutes should be sufficient.

The meditations that follow are provided only to help group participants use this prayer form, but note that *lectio* is intended to bring one to a place of prayerful contemplation where the Word of God speaks to the hearer from his or her heart. See page 11 for further instruction.

Paul's Love for Israel (9:1–5)

Christianity has its roots in Judaism. Just as Paul could not reject his ancestry and beliefs, so we cannot reject the ancient heritage of Christianity. Because we believe in Christianity's link with Judaism, Christians accept the Old Testament as the inspired Word of God. And this foundation enables us to understand many of the nuances of the New Testament and to understand the teachings of Jesus a little better, since Jesus himself was a devoted Jew. God, as a God of history, reveals God's presence through the history of God's people in both the Old and New Testaments. For this reason, Christians have a need to know the total message of the Scriptures in order to fully understand God's plan in creation.

✠ *What can I learn from this passage?*

God's Free Choice (9:6–24)

Attempting to understand the mind of God in creation is daunting. Paul shows that God does not follow human norms in creation. Rather, God has a plan for creation, and chooses whom God wishes to choose to enact this plan. Paul tells us that God chose Moses and hardened the heart of the Pharaoh in the conflict between Moses and the Egyptians. Most spiritual writers today would not accept a viewpoint that God planned every step of creation, making evil people one way and good people an-other; rather, God grants us free will. In choosing us, God does not force us to perform our call in an evil or good manner. Instead, we are free to respond to God's call as we choose—for evil or good. We are invited by the Spirit of God to choose the path that leads to life.

✠ *What can I learn from this passage?*

Witness the Prophets (9:25–33)

In the Gospel of Luke, Jesus tells the wonderful story of the lost son who returns home and is received with love by his father. His older brother, however, refuses to accept him back into the family. In fact, according to the story, the older brother complains that he has remained faithful and obedient for years and received nothing in return. The problem with the older son is that he has obeyed the rules, but he lacked the forgiving and loving spirit of the father. Paul could be agreeing with Jesus' message when he implies that some of the Israelites are acting without love and faith, like the elder son. They keep the rules, but their heart is far from God.

✠ *What can I learn from this passage?*

Faith in Christ (10:1–13)

As a former Jew in love with the Law of Moses, Paul continues to show concern for the Israelites, but his faith in Jesus as the Christ leads him to conclude that the Law has come to an end and faith in Christ has taken its place. The risen Lord has come, which means that basing one's hope for the coming of a future Messiah is futile, since Christ has already come. No one can bring Christ from heaven to earth again, nor can anyone bring Christ to rise again. It has all happened as predicted by the Law and the prophets. The reality of faith in one Lord means that the Jews and the Gentiles must share in a common worship in the one true God, for there is one God and Lord who brings salvation to all.

✠ *What can I learn from this passage?*

Faith Comes Through Hearing (10:14—11:10)

When Jesus preached parables, he said at one point, "Whoever has ears to hear ought to hear" (Mark 4:9). Although many saintly men and women preach about the message of God's love for all people, there are some who hear their message and refuse to accept it. Having ears to hear does not depend on one's physical ability, but the ability and willingness to hear with faith. Paul realizes that the message of Jesus has need for some to preach it, but he also realizes that those who listen to the preachers must be open to hearing the message. Since the prophets of the Old Testament predicted that the Israelites would not accept the message about Jesus, Paul is not surprised when the Israelites, the Chosen People, fail to acknowledge the message that was being preached to them. God's word continues to be preached today, and like the ancient Israelites and Gentiles, willingness to hear still depends on one's ability to listen with faith-filled desire and openness to the good news of Jesus our Lord.

✠ *What can I learn from this passage?*

PART 2: INDIVIDUAL STUDY (ROMANS 11)

Day 1: The Remnant of Israel (11:1–10)

Paul continues to respond to those who feel that God abandoned the Israelites, using himself as an example; he is a Jew, a descendant of Abraham, a member of the tribe of Benjamin, and one who has been chosen to believe in the message about Jesus. God knew that some of the Israelites would respond to the call, and Paul further teaches that he is not the only Israelite who believes in Jesus. He uses an incident from the Old Testament to teach this message. In 1 Kings 19, Elijah complains that he is the only Israelite true to the Lord, but God assures him that there is a remnant of 7,000 throughout Israel who still worship the true God. Paul encourages his readers by telling them that a remnant of the Israelites of his own day have accepted Jesus. This gift came to them through the grace of God, and not through their own works.

The Israelites who rejected Christ "became blind." Paul quotes from the Scriptures to show that this blindness was expected (Deuteronomy 29:4; Isaiah 29:10; Psalm 69:22–23). Although God did not force the Israelites into blindness, God permitted it to happen. In this way, Paul can say that this was the will of God.

Lectio Divina

Spend 8 to 10 minutes in silent contemplation of the following passage:

There is a famous story about Jesus entering heaven and meeting the angels at the time of his ascension. The excited angels congratulate Jesus on his successful mission and ask whom he has left behind to continue his work. Jesus tells them that he left behind a handful of disciples filled with faith and courage. Suddenly, the angels look perplexed and doubtful. They ask with some hesitation, "And Jesus, what is plan B." Jesus replies, "There is no plan B."

Jesus left behind a remnant to carry on his mission, and we are part of that remnant. We are plan A, and it is God's intention to use our little ways to do great things. The message in this passage concerning the Israelites could easily be applied to us today. We have been gifted with faith, and are called to share this faith with others. If we do not live by faith, it is not because Christ has rejected us but rather we have failed to be faithful to Christ. Looking at the small number of disciples Jesus left behind when he ascended, we might recall that no remnant of Christians in an area can be so small that it cannot change the world.

✠ *What can I learn from this passage?*

Day 2: Salvation for the Gentiles (11:11–24)

Paul turns his attention to the question of whether the Israelites have hope of recovering their call in the future. Although Paul views the failure of the Israelites to accept Christ as an occasion for Gentile salvation, he states that the Jews have not cut themselves off from faith in Jesus forever. Paul tried to preach to the Israelites about Christ, but they rejected his message and so he turned to the Gentiles, many of whom accepted this message. One might see Paul's hope for the Israelites as he notes that if their faults brought so much good, how much more would come from their acceptance of Christ?

Paul writes to the Romans, telling them of the glory he experiences in preaching to them. He seems to be saying that the purpose of his mission is to force the Israelites to become jealous and have a change of heart. Though Paul does not actually preach to the Gentiles to make them jealous, he shares that he would accept this role if it led to the Israelites' conversion. Paul is concerned for all, Gentiles as well as Jews, and he wishes all to be saved.

Furthermore, Paul repeats his previous statement about the good that has come from the Israelite rejection of Christ. If their rejection brought a reconciliation of all people to God, how much more will their acceptance bring to the world? Paul sees this acceptance as "bringing life from death." This may refer to a movement from spiritual death to spiritual life for the Israelites and all people touched by them. Likewise, Paul makes a reference to the first fruits that affect a whole mass of dough. He most likely is referring to the Israelite people who have already accepted Christ. These Christian Israelites are the remnant positively affecting the entire Israelite nation.

As Paul continues his message, he uses the image of a root and its branches. The root that is consecrated points to the patriarchs and the people of ancient Israel who were chosen by God. These holy people will continue to have an influence on all those who share in the source of God's call. The Gentiles are like wild olive branches grafted on to this root, and they share in the blessings that come from these people of the promise. Paul reminds the Gentiles that they receive their blessings from this root, and that the root did not receive its blessings from them. Therefore, Paul warns them against any boasting, reminding them that they, the wild branches, could just as easily be cut off from the root if they become proud and lose faith. If God did not hesitate to cut off the natural branches (Israelites) because of their lack of faith, so God will not hesitate to cut off the wild branches, if necessary.

Urging the Gentiles to ponder continually this action of God that led to a harsh judgment for those who rejected faith and provided a gift for those who accepted faith, Paul instructs all not to lose faith; for if they lose faith, the Gentiles can easily be cut off. Likewise, if the Israelites turn to faith in Christ, they will easily be grafted back onto the root. So Paul instructs that if the wild branch can so easily be grafted on to the root, then it must be quite simple for the Lord to graft on the natural branch—good news for the children of the promise.

Lectio Divina

Spend 8 to 10 minutes in silent contemplation of the following passage:

Paul has developed a universal view of Christ's mission. If the Gentiles, who were not the Chosen People throughout the Old Testament period, accepted faith in Christ and brought about such an abundance of blessings to the world, imagine how much more the Israelites would have brought to creation if they believed in Jesus as the Christ. Jesus said to his disciples, "I am the vine, you are the branches" (John 15:15). Paul wishes to see Jews as well as Gentiles sharing in faith in Jesus Christ. In the Old Testament, the Chosen People were the Israelites. In the New Testament, all who believe in Jesus and accept baptism are the new Chosen People. Being chosen is not enough. We must live up to our call to live as baptized Christians. Just as the old branches of the Israelites who persecuted Jesus could be cut off from the root, which is God, so baptized Christians who do not live their faith can be cut off from Christ. Paul stresses the gift of universal salvation given to all, but he also warns that this gift demands dedication and commitment. We are privileged to be one of the Chosen People through baptism, but we must live that commitment in the daily activities of our lives.

✠ *What can I learn from this passage?*

Day 3: God's Loving Mercy (11:25–36)

Paul admits to his readers that he is speaking about a mystery. Although he cannot explain the mystery, he can nevertheless tell them about it so that they will not live in ignorance. The Israelites have entered a state of blindness in their refusal to accept faith in Christ. This blindness will remain until a designated number of Gentiles (Paul does not state how many) are brought to faith in Jesus. Then all of Israel will be saved. Paul quotes from Isaiah (59:20–21; 27:9) showing that God foretold the day when all of Israel will be saved and reminds the Gentiles that the rejection of Christ on the part of the Jews has resulted in a gift for the Gentiles. But God cannot reject the Jews: they are still the "Chosen People," deeply loved by God because of the patriarchs of old and God's unconditional love for them.

Having expressed in these chapters the great mysteries of God's plan of salvation, Paul bursts out with a hymn of praise for the wonders of God. The depth of the riches, the wisdom, the knowledge, the judgments, and the ways of God are far beyond our human limitations. Paul quotes from the Scriptures in praise of God whom no one is able to counsel or comprehend (Wisdom 9:13; Isaiah 40:13). And he finally ends by proclaiming all things are from, through, and for God. All glory belongs to God forever.

Lectio Divina

Spend 8 to 10 minutes in silent contemplation of the following passage:

Paul admits that he is speaking of a mystery that he does not understand, yet attempts to explain so that his readers will not remain totally ignorant of God's plan for creation offered from Paul's perspective. The blindness of the Israelites regarding Jesus offers an opportunity to the Gentiles to accept Christ. Paul praises God, admitting that the ways of God are far beyond our human abilities to comprehend. Speaking from a viewpoint developed through his faith, Paul believes that God will not abandon God's Chosen People. He leaves us with a hopeful message saying that all of creation comes from God, remains in existence through God, and has as its goal eternal praise of God. Paul's optimistic faith is infectious; by recalling his words, we might begin to trust that God's creation is indeed moving toward a surprising fulfillment into the embrace and love of Christ for all people.

✠ *What can I learn from this passage?*

Review Questions

1. How are our attitudes today affected by the image of a Jewish remnant of converts? What is meant in Scripture by remnant?

2. In what way did the Israelites' rejection of Christianity help influence its growth? Explain.

3. Consider some instances in salvation history where God has been faithful to the covenant. How has God been faithful to you throughout your life (this year, this week, or this day)?

LESSON 5

The Duties of Christians

ROMANS 12—16

None of us lives for oneself, and no one dies for oneself. For if we live, we live for the Lord, and if we die, we die for the Lord; so then, whether we live or die, we are the Lord's (14:7—8).

Opening Prayer (SEE PAGE 20)

Context

Part 1: Romans 12:1—14 Paul urges his readers to offer themselves as living sacrifices and not to align themselves with the attitudes of the age in which they live. He portrays the Church as a body, the Body of Christ, with each one having special and unique gifts for the good of the community, which they are encouraged to use for the benefit of all. Furthermore, Paul encourages Christians to follow the directives of civil authority, viewing those in authority as ministers of God. They should show love for all, including those who persecute them, realizing that love is the fulfillment of the law.

Part 2: Romans 15—16 In Paul's day, there were many Jewish Christians who were struggling with the transition from Judaism to living as followers of Christ; and likewise there were many from among the Gentiles who were struggling to rid themselves of pagan beliefs and practices. Paul accuses them all as being "weak in faith," since they are still haunted by past beliefs and rituals.

Though his words may appear harsh, he gently urges his readers to patiently endure the actions of those who are weak in faith so that all may glorify God with one voice.

He continues his message by explaining that Christ became a minister to the Israelites to fulfill the promises of God, and to the Gentiles that they may praise God. Paul claims that he boasts, not about himself, but about God's choice of him to be an apostle to the Gentiles; and adds that he longed to arrive at Rome on his way to Spain. He ends by sending greetings to those he knows in Rome and a warning to the church at Rome not to allow dissension among themselves to grow and wreak havoc within the community.

PART 1: GROUP STUDY (ROMANS 12—14)

Read aloud Romans 12—14.

12:1–8 A Living Sacrifice

Paul urges the Romans to live their Christianity by becoming living sacrifices, offering a holy and pleasing form of worship to God through their lives. Just as the offering of animal sacrifice was given to God in Old Testament times as a gift acceptable to God, so Paul now motivates his readers to replace this offering with their own life of service. This is the new, acceptable sacrifice that becomes holy because of God's mercy.

In offering this gift, Paul urges his listeners not to conform themselves to the ways of the age in which they live, but to rise above these ways and to live according to God's will. Because they cannot live according to the will of God without a special gift from God, they must open their minds and hearts to God's generosity. In this way, their lives will be able to discern God's will for them and therefore be transformed. Paul heard of the immoral practices and attitudes of many Romans, realizing the difficulties faced by Christians living in such an atmosphere.

Paul warns Christians not to think too highly of themselves, but to judge themselves honestly in accordance with their faith. He uses the image of a body to describe Christian membership and unity within the Body of Christ. This membership demands response, but a Christian should not pride himself or herself on gifts received. The gifts are given for the good of the body, and just as a body has many members that perform their own particular functions for the health of the body, so the members of the Body of Christ must perform their functions well for the sake of others. The gifts of prophecy, ministry, teaching, almsgiving, leadership, and compassion are all important to the Body of Christ. Paul urges his readers to use their gifts as perfectly as possible for the good of others.

12:9–21 One Body With Many Parts

Paul gives short maxims to tell his readers how they should live. They should love deeply and sincerely, a practice that will ward off evil and hold them fast to what is good. In other words, this attitude of love will show in their actions, which are listed by Paul in this passage. Our love for one another should be like the comfort found in loving families. It should not only respond to requests from others, but it should also anticipate the needs of others and respect their dignity. One should avoid growing weak in zeal, act with the fervor that comes from the Spirit, and realize that all service is ultimately service to the Lord.

This love demands joyful hope, patient endurance, and constant prayer. Christians should receive others with a loving hospitality, identifying the needs of others and responding as if those needs were our own. Even those who persecute Christians should receive a blessing in turn for their evil. True Christians enter so deeply into the needs of others that they rejoice or weep as others rejoice or weep, and they treat others, of every class, with the same dignity, without seeking any gain for themselves. They neither overestimate their own wisdom, nor do they injure those who have injured them. And they strive to live honorably and peacefully with all. Although Paul exhorts his readers to act in this manner, he actually presumes that this is the way for Christians to live.

Paul gives his final list in this passage by drawing his message from the Old Testament Book of Proverbs (25:21–22). Revenge belongs only to God who, as the creator and giver of gifts, has a right to vengeance. Kindness will be far more painful to one's enemies than torture. If an enemy is hungry or thirsty, Christians should respond to those needs. In this way, Christians conquer evil by using their goodness as a proper weapon.

13:1–7 All Authority From God

Paul begins this passage by directing his readers to obey human authority because it comes from God. Rebellion against such authority, therefore, is also rebellion against God. When Paul wrote this letter, he would have known of no apparent reason to reject the authority of Rome. In the Acts of the Apostles, he himself appeals to this authority to avoid an unjust trial in Jerusalem (25:1–12). Persecution of the Christians at Rome took place at a later date, after Paul had written Romans. The Zealots of Paul's day would not have condoned his words concerning acceptance of authority, because they believed that no outside authority had the right to rule the Jewish nation. According to Paul, only those who disobey this authority need fear, because they will receive punishment. The way to avoid fearing any authority is to do what is right. The ruler, as a servant of God, has the right to inflict punishment on those disobeying a just law.

Not only for the sake of the law, but also for the sake of conscience, Christians should obey true authority. Paul includes the paying of taxes as just, because the ruler needs support and has a right to wages. In following Christ, many Christians may have misinterpreted the freedom from sin that Paul teaches as freedom from all human authority. Lest Christians become a source of rebellion and destruction in a society in need of guidance, Paul stresses this need for faithful obedience to human authority.

13:8–14 Love Fulfills the Law

The paying of one's debt to support the rulers in the last passage is linked to this passage. The debt is now an internal debt owed by Christians to others, namely, the call to love one another. This love fulfills the Law (Torah) that is in the commandments and may be summed up with the words from the Book of Leviticus in the Old Testament, which call us to love our neighbor as oneself (19:18). In doing this, one fulfills all laws.

Paul sees the days in which the world is living as the "last days"—the days in which the grace of Christ has come upon creation. Although he does not expect the Second Coming to take place immediately, as he did during the early days of his ministry, Paul still believes that the day of salvation is coming soon, and reminds Christians that the works of darkness have come to an end. It is now time to put on the armor of light.

Paul lists the sinful deeds that he believes are symbols of actions performed in darkness, and urges his readers to live honorably in the light of day. An image is recalled of how Christ clothed us at baptism, so Paul now urges his readers to "put on the Lord Jesus Christ" and to make no provisions for the sinful desires of this world.

14:1–12 To Live and Die for Christ

Not all converts to Christianity overcome lifelong practices. Paul recognizes this and addresses those who are "weak" in the faith and those who are "strong" in the faith. Although Paul warns them not to judge one another, he inadvertently judges those who are slow to accept the full changes brought about by Christianity, calling them "weak in faith." He warns the "strong in faith" not to enter into debates with the weak and not to flaunt their right to eat whenever they wish. Instead, they should have regard for those who abstain from certain foods, and those who abstain from these foods should not judge those who do not. Paul warns both groups that they are like slaves who belong to the Lord, their master. Because of this, they have no right to judge another slave. Only the master (the Lord) has that right. Some will eat to honor the Lord, while others will not eat to honor the Lord. God allows people to show honor through their chosen actions as long as they are following the convictions of their hearts.

Through his death and resurrection, Jesus has become the Lord of both the dead and the living. In life and in death, we belong to the Lord; this means that we do not have the right to judge another. This right belongs to the Lord alone, before whom all must appear on the day of judgment. Through their words (praise from the tongues) and actions (bending the knee in homage), all will acknowledge the Lord. The basic message Paul teaches is one of mutual respect between those of differing opinions concerning the manner in which they show honor to God.

Paul recognizes that because people must give an account before God for themselves, Christians should strive to help others live according to their conscience, rather than confuse or hinder them. Paul believes, along with the "strong in faith," that the authority of Jesus Christ has determined that nothing is unclean in itself; rather, for the person who believes something to be unclean, it is for that person. In this instance, keep in mind that Paul is trying to reconcile Gentile and Israelite traditions in order to unify early Christians.

The strong in faith should neither ridicule another for abstaining from certain foods nor eat the food that is allowed if it will cause scandal for another. It is not the freedom of eating and drinking that makes up the kingdom of God, but it is the justice, peace, and joy that come from the Spirit. The true Christian is one who sets his or her mind on bringing about peace, working to strengthen the faith of others.

Paul warns the Christians of strong faith not to flaunt this right to eat unclean foods, but instead encourages them to sacrifice all rights to eat these foods so as to avoid causing any type of scandal that could weaken the faith of another. The gift of faith should be used as a guide for one's life rather than a rod to cause another difficulties. All must follow their own conscience. Even if they do what is allowed (while believing that it is not permissible), they are guilty of acting against their conscience.

Review Questions

1. How can we become a living sacrifice, holy and pleasing to God?

2. What does the image of the Church as the Body of Christ tell us about the Church and our membership or role within it?

3. Do you find it difficult to love as Paul directs us to love in Romans (12:9–21)? Why or why not?

4. What would Paul say about our need to respect civil authorities today? Does this affect your attitude toward these systems? Explain.

5. Does an awareness of the last days help us to live a better life? If so, how?

6. How would you apply Paul's advice about love and consideration for the weak in faith to your life today?

Closing Prayer (SEE PAGE 20)

Pray the closing prayer now or after *lectio divina*.

Lectio Divina (SEE PAGE 11)

Relax your body and maintain a posture of prayer (back straight, eyes shut, feet flat on the floor). This exercise can take as long as you want, but in the context of this Bible study, 10 to 20 minutes should be sufficient.

The meditations that follow are provided only to help group participants use this prayer form, but note that *lectio* is intended to bring one to a place of prayerful contemplation where the Word of God speaks to the hearer from his or her heart. See page 11 for further instruction.

A Living Sacrifice (12:1–8)

Paul has already proven his dedication to God when he writes his Letter to the Romans, and now he urges all Christians to do the same. His message applies to us as much as it does to the people of his own age. We are to be a new form of sacrifice and must dedicate our lives to serving God. We are not to conform ourselves to worldly attitudes of the age in which we live, but are to open ourselves to the will of God in our lives. Instead of bragging about our gifts, we are to realize that we have received our gifts from God for the sake of the Body of Christ on earth. Whatever gifts we have received, they depend on God's work in our lives to become effective, and God depends on us to use them wisely and well.

✠ *What can I learn from this passage?*

One Body With Many Parts (12:9–21)

Paul lists practical virtues involved in living as a Christian that sound like proverbs for living well. He speaks wisely of the virtue of love, which is the centerpiece of Jesus' message in the gospels. He tells us that we should live with love as the foundation of our lives, love as strong as that found in families. It consists in an energetic love for others and a respect for the dignity of others. Love not only demands hope, endurance, and constant prayer, but also looks to the needs of those who love us and hurt us. It consists in becoming one with others in their joys and sorrows, and in seeking the good of others over any gain we may receive from them. Revenge should be left to God, and our enemies should be treated with love. In short, all Christians should dedicate themselves to loving everyone without counting the cost.

✠ *What can I learn from this passage?*

An Authority From God (13:1–7)

Bishops throughout the world urge Catholics in their country to support and obey a lawful government as long as it does not interfere with our Catholic teaching. Paul continues his list of virtues as he now addresses civic virtues, urging his readers to be faithful to lawful authority. He views rebellion against lawful authority as a rebellion against God, and he notes that the lawful ruler, as a servant of God, has the right to inflict punishment where necessary. Since the government needs funds for ministry, paying taxes is just. Paul believes that we as Christians must in good conscience perform our duties as citizens under the leadership of lawful authority. Paul is teaching the commonly accepted Christian message concerning the performance of our civic duties. In doing this, we are not only helping lawful authority, but helping those being served by this authority.

✠ *What can I learn from this passage?*

Love Fulfills the Law (13:8–14)

Paul views those who lack love as living in darkness. It is now time for us to put on the armor of light and live in an honorable manner. Paul reiterates the call for us to love one another, clothing ourselves in Christ and living with the attitude of Jesus Christ, which is one of love for all people. Clothing ourselves in Christ recalls our baptism, when we put on the Lord Jesus Christ and live free from the sinful allurements of the world. Paul's belief and hope are that we, who fully understand the importance of clothing ourselves in Christ in baptism, will live fully in the light of Jesus.

✠ *What can I learn from this passage?*

To Live and Die for Christ (14:1–12)

Paul stresses two virtues in this passage. He warns against judging others who have just begun their journey in the faith and who are thus still weak, and he calls those with strong faith to be considerate of those who are less strong so as not cause scandal by doing what is permitted. Paul praises those who are following their conscience, whether they believe they can eat what is permitted or certain foods they are not permitted to eat. When the strong in faith abstain for the sake of those who are weak, they are establishing justice, peace, and joy in the community, which are more important than proving that one is right and the other is wrong. Paul considers mutual respect to be a major Christian virtue.

✠ *What can I learn from this passage?*

PART 2: INDIVIDUAL STUDY (ROMANS 15—16)

Day 1: Living in Harmony (15:1–13)

Paul identifies himself with the strong in faith and urges them to bear with the weak (as he also must do). They should not seek their own satisfaction, but that of their neighbors, encouraging them by their way of life. He points to Christ as an example of selfless giving by applying to him the words of Psalm 69:9, which originally applied to the difficulties faced by the psalmist in his concern for the Jewish Temple. Just as Christ accepted abuse for the sake of others, so the strong in faith should be willing to accept the same form of abuse. Paul believes that the Scriptures are meant to be a source of instruction for the people of faith; they are words of encouragement to remain patiently firm in the practice of faith that leads to hope.

Paul's address becomes a prayer. He prays that God, who is the source of firm faith and encouragement, will bring all Christians to harmony with one another in the Spirit of Jesus Christ. In this way, all Christians will fulfill the call of praising God, the Father of our Lord Jesus Christ, with one voice. This unity of praise is essential to Christianity.

Paul continues to exhort his readers to reach out in love to one another in the same manner by which Christ reached out to welcome all for the glory of God. Because God must remain faithful to the promise made to the Israelites, Christ willingly became a slave to the Jews. Paul seems to imply that God made the promise of a Messiah to the patriarchs, but this is not true. The promise of the Messiah came later in the history of the Israelite nation. Many writers of Paul's day, however, saw this promise of a Messiah as implicit in the promises made to Abraham, Isaac, and Jacob. Christ thus fulfilled this role that was promised by God to the Israelites.

The Gentiles, who did not receive the promise, glorify God for the mercy shown to them. Paul makes use of a series of texts from the Old Testament that speaks of this mercy of God toward the Gentiles (Psalm 18:49; Deuteronomy 32:43; Psalm 117:1; Isaiah 11:10), praying that his readers will be filled with the deep joy and peace that come from belief in Christ. The basis of this joy and peace is the hope that comes to them through the power of the Spirit.

Lectio Divina

Spend 8 to 10 minutes in silent contemplation of the following passage:

Paul's motive in addressing the strong in faith in this manner is his concern for harmony in the community. So he prays for the community, asking God who is the source of all faith and harmony to bring encouragement to them so that they may live in the Spirit of Christ. Since the community is called to praise God with one voice, living in harmony enables them to fulfill this call; one rightly viewed by Paul as essential to Christianity. Our call as Christians is first to learn to express love for one another as Jesus expressed love for us. For Jesus was willing to bind himself to the dictates of the Mosaic Law for the sake of the promise God made to the Jews, and God reached out to the Gentiles through Christ Jesus. All Christians must express gratitude to God for God's gifts given freely to Jews and Gentiles alike, for we all share in God's blessings.

✠ *What can I learn from this passage?*

Day 2: Apostle to the Gentiles (15:14–33)

Paul begins this passage by praising the goodness and knowledge of the Roman Christians, and by recognizing that they are thus able to instruct one another in the faith. This praise of the Romans may have also stemmed from Paul's desire to be favorably received by them. Despite these qualities, Paul has dared to write to the Romans because of the special call he has received from Jesus Christ: the call to be an apostle to the Gentiles. He further understands this ministry as a priestly call that allows him to act as a priest offering the Gentiles to God as a holy and acceptable sacrifice. Paul recognizes that his ministry, like that of Jesus, is made effective through the power of the Holy Spirit. Paul can boast, not because of the work he has done, but because of the work that Jesus Christ has performed through him. He admits that the miraculous signs he performed came about through the power of the Spirit of God working through him.

Paul expresses his belief that he has completed his mission to share the message from Jerusalem to Illyricum and other points in between. In this ministry, Paul has made a point never to preach where another had laid the foundation in the faith, and in this way to spread the word of Christ as far as possible. He makes use of the words of Isaiah (52:15), who foretold that those who have never heard of Jesus will see and understand the Lord. He wishes to share the Word with those who have not yet heard about Christ.

Because of this need to spread the Word to these areas, Paul tells the Romans that he has been unable to visit them. Now, as he turns his apostolate in another direction, toward Spain, he hopes to fulfill an ambition of many years in finally being with them for a short time. Before he begins this journey to Rome, he must first deliver to Jerusalem the collection taken up among the Gentiles for the Jerusalem church. He tells his readers that the Gentiles did this on their own, as a sign of gratitude and as an effort to make some return for the spiritual gifts they had received from Jerusalem. Paul intends to bring the collection to Jerusalem and then to set out for Spain, stopping at Rome along the way.

Paul hints at the difficulties that he fears he will encounter in Jerusalem. The Book of the Acts of the Apostles tells of the warnings given to Paul by his friends as he makes this journey. He now asks the Roman Christians to pray for him that he may avoid any encounters with the Jews who do not accept Christ and that the Jewish Christians will favorably receive his offering from the Gentiles. Paul again expresses his desire to be with the Romans and wishes them the customary greeting of peace in the Lord.

Lectio Divina

Spend 8 to 10 minutes in silent contemplation of the following passage:

> The aim of Christianity is to recognize the unity of all Christians throughout the world, and the ministry of the Spirit of God working within each one of us. Paul's boast is never about himself, but always about the Spirit of the Lord working through him. He recognizes his call as an apostle to the Gentiles and views himself as offering his ministry to God as an acceptable sacrifice, worthy of God. This offering is not generated from him directly, but from the Spirit working through him. Throughout his ministry, Paul shows a universal concern for the Church and desires to share Christ's word with those who have not heard it. Whatever we do as Christians, whether in prayer or through our good works, it is important to recall that our help comes from the promptings of the Spirit who guides and inspires us.

✠ *What can I learn from this passage?*

Day 3: Greetings (16:1–24)

In Paul's time, travelers often needed a letter of recommendation in order to gain acceptance in a community. Paul sends such a letter (perhaps this letter) to the Romans with Phoebe, whom he calls a deacon, and urges them to receive her with love.

Paul sends his greeting to Prisca and Aquila, two companions who appear with him several times in the Acts of the Apostles (see Acts 18:1ff). While in Corinth, Paul lived in the home of Prisca and Aquila and shared with them the same profession of tent-making. They had come from Rome when the emperor Claudius banished all Jews from that area. When Paul went on to Ephesus, they traveled with him. Paul not only sends his greetings to them but also to all who meet in their house.

Next, Paul greets Epaenetus, the first convert from Asia in an area near Ephesus. From this fact and the mention of the home of Aquila and Prisca, many commentators believe that this greeting at the end of the letter to the Romans properly belongs at the end of a letter to the people of Ephesus. Another reason some commentators attribute this ending to a letter to the people of Ephesus lies in the number of people to whom Paul sends his greetings. He seems to know many people at Rome, which would hardly be the case if he had never visited the area. All are urged to greet one another with the affection of true disciples. Paul adds a greeting from all the churches of Christ, thus showing the concern of Christians for one another.

Paul warns his readers against those who would lead to dissensions and offenses, declaring that they should be avoided because they do not serve Christ but themselves. With their oratorical skills, they are able to deceive the "simple-minded." Perhaps Paul has received news about such people in Rome. Another explanation is that these lines are truly an ending to a letter to Ephesus, where such problems have already occurred.

Still, Paul commends them for their obedience—namely, for their manner of living the faith. He makes an allusion to the serpent of Genesis (3:15), identified as the devil in the Book of Wisdom (2:24), whom God crushes under their feet, and ends this passage by wishing his readers the blessings of the Lord Jesus Christ.

In common practice, an author of a letter would send greetings from those with him. Paul sends greetings from Timothy, whom we know from the Acts of the Apostles, and from others whose activities we do not know. The author of a letter was not always the writer of the letter. In this case, Paul has apparently dictated his letter to Tertius, who now sends his own greetings to the Romans.

Lectio Divina

Spend 8 to 10 minutes in silent contemplation of the following passage:

Although the ending of the letter may not have been originally part of Paul's letter to the Romans, it teaches a message central to Paul's concern for the Christian community. He warns against dissensions that some seem to encourage through their oratorical skills. As found earlier in his Letter to the Romans, Paul strives to encourage harmony in the community and urges his readers to avoid all forms of judging or scandalizing others, especially those who are new to the faith. The message of Paul continues to apply to us today. As Christians, we strive to share the message of Jesus not only through our words but also through our deeds. Love and harmony among the members of the Christian community can have a great influence in bringing others to faith in Christ.

✠ *What can I learn from this passage?*

Day 4: Praise for God (16:25–27)

The letter ends with a doxology, which most commentators doubt was written by Paul. The letters of Paul do not usually end with a doxology, and the style and language of this ending do not match that of the rest of the letter. This doxology praises God through Jesus Christ for all ages. It speaks of the glory of God, who is all-wise and who is able to strengthen all in the message of the gospel preached by Paul. Although the Old Testament prophets spoke of this age of fulfillment in Christ, they could not truly understand this mystery that had been hidden until now. Because this message has come to the Gentiles, who accept this gospel and live by faith, the writer offers this praise to God.

Lectio Divina

Spend 8 to 10 minutes in silent contemplation of the following passage:

Although commentators question Paul's writing of the ending of this Letter to the Romans, the content does not stray from the teaching of Paul. The author praises God for the many gifts given through Jesus Christ, especially those given to the Gentiles. It continues to recognize the universal call for salvation in Christ found in Paul's letters. For us, it illustrates God's loving concern for all people, and not just for a limited amount of people or a particular nation. The letter teaches that Christ came for all people.

✠ *What can I learn from this passage?*

Review Questions

1. How can we apply to our own lives Paul's words concerning Christ's willingness to please others rather than himself?

2. Why do we all feel a need to ask others to pray for us, as Paul did?

3. What lesson can we learn from Paul's need for support from his friends in spreading Christ's message? In what ways do your friends encourage you to live the gospel message?

4. What ripple effect did dissension among early Christians create?

Loyalty to the Gospel

GALATIANS 1–3

For through faith you are all children of God in Christ Jesus. For all of you who were baptized into Christ have clothed yourselves with Christ (Galatians 3:26–27).

> **Suggestion to Participants:** Re-read the "Introduction to Letters to the Romans and Galatians" on page 21 as you prepare to study lessons 6 and 7.

Opening Prayer (SEE PAGE 20)

Context

Part 1: Galatians 1—2:10 Paul introduces himself as an apostle chosen by Jesus, sending greetings to the church at Galatia and offering peace and grace from the Lord. The beginning of the passage is curt, as Paul immediately expresses his surprise that they have so easily abandoned the gospel he taught them in order to accept a different gospel. In fact, he curses those who taught them a different gospel and maintains that it would be equally false if it were to be presented by angels. Defending the gospel that he preaches, Paul notes that it does not come from human origin, but from God. By recalling for his readers his own conversion and call to preach among the Gentiles, he magnifies the transforming effect of the gospel on humanity, leading many in the community to glorify God.

Part 2: Galatians 2:11—3 Paul tells how he openly confronted Peter who was eating with Gentiles, but left them when some Jewish Christians arrived. When Peter left the Gentiles to eat with the Jews, Paul asked Peter in front of all how he who was living like a Gentile could compel Gentiles to live like Jews. Since Peter was giving an example of freedom from the law to the Gentiles, those Gentiles who had accepted Christ would become confused when Peter suddenly began to eat like a Jew. Paul later adds that Christians are not justified by works of the law, but by faith in Jesus Christ. If following Christ means that they are living in sin, then Christ would be a minister of sin, which is a foolish thought. It is Christ who lives in the baptized Christian. If the law is still in effect, then Christ died for nothing. Paul refers to Abraham as an example of living by faith instead of the Law. Through faith, we are children of God.

PART 1: GROUP STUDY (GALATIANS 1—2:10)

Read aloud Galatians 1—2:10.

1:1–5 Greeting

The intent of this letter immediately influences the opening greeting. Paul is writing to the Galatians, who have accepted the contrary gospel of the Judaizers, so he must first identify the source of his own authority. So he declares that he is an apostle whose call and authority come from Jesus Christ and God the Father, the Holy One responsible for raising Jesus from the dead. It is important for Paul to state that his call as an apostle does not come from human authority, since he was not a witness to the life of Jesus, nor did he learn his gospel from those who were followers of Christ. Paul implies that the Judaizers cannot claim any divine authority for their message.

Paul follows the usual format used in the opening of letters in his day. He identifies himself, names the audience for whom the letter is

intended, and sends them greetings. He writes to the "churches of Galatia," inferring that he is writing to more than one community; and
offers the usual well wishes of grace and peace that come from God and
Jesus Christ. The companions whose greetings he sends along with his
own are not named here.

When Paul names Jesus Christ in his greeting, he subtly lays the
foundation of the argument in his letter. Jesus, in accordance with the
will of God the Father, is the one who suffered and died for our sins to
rescue us from the evils of the present age; and Paul includes the practices of the Mosaic Law among those things from which we have been
rescued. Because of these blessings brought about by the action of Jesus,
Paul offers him eternal praise.

1:6–10 Loyalty to the Gospel

Paul noticeably omits to offer thanksgiving for those addressed, as he
does in his other letters. It is difficult to determine the length of time
between Paul's visit to this particular audience and the writing of this
letter. It may have been several months or several years, but, whatever
the time, Paul is amazed that the Galatians could have accepted another
"gospel" in so short a time, and therefore emphatically exhorts that there
is only one gospel. Paul, of course, is speaking of the Gospel of Jesus
Christ, which calls for freedom from the practices of the Mosaic Law,
especially circumcision.

Recognizing that the Judaizers have confused the Galatians with their
preaching about the Mosaic practices, Paul curses anyone who preaches
a gospel different from the one he shared with them (even if this person
were to be an angel). For the sake of emphasis, he repeats this message
twice. Furthermore, Paul openly expresses his concern for the gospel of
Jesus Christ, even though the Galatians would possibly snub him for his
rejection of the new gospel they had begun to accept as a replacement for
the gospel Paul preached. Even if he must pay the price of being dishon-
ored in their sight, Paul states that he will never stop serving Christ. It is
possible that some of the Judaizers may have accused Paul of softening
the gospel demands for the sake of adding more converts. So his strong

response to the situation illustrates merely that he has no intention of seeking favor by watering down the gospel.

By the time he finishes the first few paragraphs of his letter, he clearly launches its overall direction. This direction indicates that Paul is not pleased with the Galatians easy acceptance of a new gospel, so he begins to teach what is false in the gospel presented by the Judaizers. Thus, as he sets out to address the issues with the false gospel, he emphasizes the value of faith in Christ.

1:11–24 Paul Defends His Mission

Despite his anger with the Galatians, Paul still considers them his brothers and sisters in Christ. The Judaizers apparently convinced the Galatians that Paul did not preach the message of Christ, but adapted the message according to his own whims. Paul does not attempt to refute any of these accusations, but rather denies he preaches a merely human gospel, and claims to receive his knowledge about Christ from revelation. This revelation seems to refer to the time of his conversion, and is not meant to be a denial of any learning gained from others about Christ and his teachings. He implies that the gospel taught by the Judaizers had a human origin. The teachings of Paul applied the message of Jesus to life in the community, and this would eventually have a major influence on the theology of the Church.

Paul recalls the zeal of his early years within Judaism when he persecuted the Church and tried to destroy it. He points out that he followed the Jewish practices to the letter. Yet, in the plan of God, Paul was destined to preach the gospel to the Gentiles. Because of this divine plan, Paul had no need for human teachers or for any direction from the church at Jerusalem. After his conversion, he set off for an area south of Damascus, which he called Arabia. He then returned to Damascus, and, after three years likely of prayer and reflection, he went to Jerusalem.

Paul speaks of visiting with Peter, whom he calls by his Aramaic name, "Cephas." The name "Cephas" and "Peter" both mean rock. The visit apparently consisted of no more than just getting acquainted. Peter and Paul shared an understanding of their teachings with each other. Paul spent only fifteen days with Peter, hardly enough time for any deep lessons in faith. At that time, the only other disciple he met was James, the head of the Jerusalem church (not James the apostle), who is referred to as the brother of Jesus in Acts of the Apostles. This reference to James as Jesus' brother may mean that he is related to Jesus in some manner for in Jesus' culture, a cousin could be referred to as one's brother.

Paul then went to Syria and Cilicia, and he describes the reaction of the Christians of Judea to his ministry. Although they did not know him personally, they heard that he was the one who had previously persecuted the Church and was now preaching the faith. They praised God for this gift, thus showing that they had accepted Paul as a true disciple of Jesus. Some of the Judean Christians would later become the ones to reject Paul's teachings and cause him to eventually turn his attention to the Gentiles.

2:1–10 The Council in Jerusalem

Fourteen years later, Paul travels to Jerusalem with Barnabas and Titus. Barnabas was a Jewish Christian and companion with Paul on his missionary endeavors. Titus was a Greek Christian who was also a companion of Paul on his missionary journeys. He goes to the leaders of the church at Jerusalem, not for the sake of gaining their approval for his teaching, but to avoid conflict between his teaching and that of the Jerusalem church. Paul states that the origin of his journey to Jerusalem came from a revelation, but the Book of Acts tells us that Paul and others were sent by the church at Antioch to resolve some differences concerning the difficulty involved in having the Gentiles follow Jewish practices, especially circumcision. Although the occasion of the visit was very possibly the Council of Jerusalem as described in Acts (15:6–12), there are differences between the events as described in this letter and those found in Acts. In this passage, Paul and Barnabas are commissioned to preach to the Gentiles.

Paul wanted to avoid conflict among the churches, and he wished to explain the direction his teaching had taken. He had hoped to avoid the very problems that arose at Galatia, where some converts from Judaism taught the need for following the Mosaic practices, while others, such as

Paul and his followers, did not. The leaders of the church at Jerusalem agreed with Paul to such an extent that they did not demand that Titus, a Greek, undergo circumcision. Even in Jerusalem, Paul had to face those who were trying to force Mosaic practices on the Gentile converts. He treats them harshly, calling them false members who were trying to take away the freedom from the Law gained by Christ. It was for the sake of the Gentiles that Paul resisted their efforts and defended the truth of the gospel.

The leaders of the church at Jerusalem were held in high regard and were important to Christians of all areas. Paul states that this honored position makes no difference to him, because God has no favorites. Paul accepts their position of importance and points out that they did not ask him to add anything to what he already told them. In fact, since these leaders recognize Paul and Barnabas' special mission to the Gentiles, they encourage them to continue this mission. Paul places himself on equal par with Peter when he declares that God, who worked through Peter in his mission to the Jews, also worked through him in his mission to the Gentiles. Paul names James, Cephas (Peter), and John as the three leaders who sent Paul and Barnabas on their mission. John, who is mentioned here, is most likely John the apostle and one of the Twelve. Although Cephas plays a central leadership role in the early community, James, as the head of the Jerusalem church, would be named first in connection with any Church decision. For the Jerusalem church held a primary position in the early years after the ascension of Jesus, and was the source for missionary activity outside of Jerusalem.

When Paul leaves Jerusalem after the council, he receives no limitation on his manner of preaching. The only stipulation was that he support the poor of the Jerusalem community, which he was already doing—not only for the sake of helping the poor, but also as an occasion to show the unity that existed between the Gentile and Jerusalem churches.

Review Questions

1. How does our call to be an apostle in the world today differ from that of Paul?

2. Why do you think that Paul mentions that Christ gave himself for our sins at the very beginning of this letter?

3. What was the difference between Paul's gospel and that of the Judaizers?

4. How does Paul's past life as a Jew influence or affect his understanding of the message of Jesus?

5. Would you consider the Judaizers true Christians? Explain.

6. What is the significance of the Council of Jerusalem for us today?

Closing Prayer (SEE PAGE 20)

Pray the closing prayer now or after *lectio divina*.

Lectio Divina (SEE PAGE 11)

Relax your body and maintain a posture of prayer (back straight, eyes shut, feet flat on the floor). This exercise can take as long as you want, but in the context of this Bible study, 10 to 20 minutes should be sufficient.

The meditations that follow are provided only to help group participants use this prayer form, but note that *lectio* is intended to bring one to a place of prayerful contemplation where the Word of God speaks to the hearer from his or her heart. See page 11 for further instruction.

Greeting (1:1–5)

Paul speaks as an apostle appointed directly by Jesus Christ who was raised from the dead. His mission, like that of many missionaries of his own day and in our world today, is not to spread turmoil, but to spread the peace and love of God which come to us from Jesus who offered himself for all of us. Paul speaks as one appointed in a miraculous manner, not as one who followed Jesus during his earthly life. Like many missionaries who preach about the love and concern of Christ, Paul must defend himself against those who would accuse him of preaching his own message. We today must remain faithful to the message of Jesus Christ which we learn from reading and understanding the Scriptures. Like Paul, we do not preach our own message but the message of Jesus the Christ, who suffered and died for our sins. The foundation for our mission in life is the same as Paul's, namely to declare good news of the gospel: the life, death, and resurrection of Jesus the Christ, the Son of God.

✠ *What can I learn from this passage?*

Loyalty to the Gospel (1:6–10)

Jesus suffered, died, and was raised that we might live and share his message of loving one another. In his missionary journeys, Paul did not strive to win friends and influence people, but remains firm in his belief that his mission comes from God. He is so firm that he is even willing to cast a curse upon angels who would disagree with the gospel message. In his manner of speaking, Paul challenges the people to judge whether he is seeking the applause of people or the favor of Jesus Christ. For in his day, he had to confront those who demanded more ritual practices of Christ's followers than Jesus himself did. So Paul's firm stance in favor of the message of the gospels becomes an example for us as we live our faith in the world today.

✠ *What can I learn from this passage?*

Paul Defends His Mission (1:11–24)

Change happens through the grace of God. Just as Jesus had to defend himself against his neighbors in Nazareth who knew his past life and could not believe he was any different from them, so Paul had to do likewise for those who could not believe that he had changed from being a persecutor of Christians to a missionary intent on spreading Jesus' message. We can receive two messages from this reading. First, we must believe that through the grace of God people can change their way of life and become deeply devoted to Christ. And the second is that we, no matter what our background, can receive a grace that can make us more devoted lovers of God. Grace can come to us at unexpected moments.

We do not live according to the image people have of our past life, but we live in the present, open to God's grace working in us.

✠ *What can I learn from this passage?*

The Council of Jerusalem (2:1–10)

Frequently change is difficult to accept, especially when it involves our attitudes toward our relationship with God. Paul speaks of his meeting with the leaders of the Christians in Jerusalem and the favorable outcome of the meeting, an outcome that allowed the Gentile converts to be baptized without being obliged to follow the Jewish laws and traditions. Despite this approval, Paul would endure rejection at the hands of those who resisted an abandonment of the change. Little did the Church realize at the time that this change would lead to a visible separation of Christianity from the Judaism of Paul's day. Paul became God's chosen apostle to the Gentiles. Unknown to the leaders of Jerusalem, the Spirit was not only providing for their own era, but for every era in the future of the Church.

✠ *What can I learn from this passage?*

Part 2: Individual Study (Galatians 2:11—3)

Day 1: Justification by Faith (2:11–14)

In the Acts of Apostles, the author tells the story of Peter receiving a vision directing him to eat food that the Jews considered unclean. Following the direction of the Lord, Peter went to the home of Cornelius, a Gentile centurion, entered his home (an act which would make a Jew like Peter unclean), and converted and baptized the whole household. He remained with the centurion and his household for a few days, obviously eating their food, although Acts does not mention this specifically. When Peter returned to Jerusalem, he had to defend his actions against the Christian Jews (see Acts 10:1—11:18). Apparently, as a result of his experience with the household of Cornelius, Peter becomes the one to defend the petition of Barnabas and Paul at the Council of Jerusalem when they requested that the Mosaic Law not be imposed on the Gentiles (see Acts 15).

Sometime after the Council of Jerusalem, when Cephas (Peter) visited Antioch for the first time, he ate with the Gentile converts without hesitation. When the rigid Jewish Christians who refused to accept the verdict of the Council of Jerusalem arrived, Cephas withdrew from eating with the Gentile Christians to dine with the party from Judea. Paul became furious with him and opposed him to his face. In his rebuke of Cephas, he recalled that Peter did not hesitate to eat previously with the Gentiles, yet he was forcing the Mosaic practices on them. To avoid scandal for the Jewish Christians from Jerusalem, Cephas was causing scandal for the Gentiles of Antioch.

Paul tells his readers that Cephas' actions were clearly wrong, and his open rebuke of Cephas underlines the importance of Cephas in the early Church community. If Cephas were simply one of the disciples, Paul would not have made such an open issue of rebuking him, but he states boldly, "And when Cephas came to Antioch, I opposed him to his face because he was clearly wrong" (2:11). He becomes even more bold when he further rebukes Cephas in front of everyone with the words: "If you, though a Jew, are living like a Gentile and not like a Jew, how can you compel the

Gentiles to live like Jews" (2:14). The rebuke of Cephas by Paul recalls an earlier event in the gospels when Jesus rebukes Peter for tempting him to avoid the suffering entailed in Jesus' mission. At that point, Jesus said to Peter, "Get behind me Satan. You are not thinking as God does, but as human beings do" (Mark 8:33). Despite his important position among Jesus' disciples, Paul felt a need to rebuke Cephas as Jesus had to rebuke him during his lifetime on earth.

Paul tells us that many Jewish converts in Antioch did the same as Cephas and, to the dismay and sadness of Paul, Barnabas joined them. Barnabas had been preaching to the Gentiles with Paul and living among them, and had already joined Paul in converting many Gentiles. He became a type of mentor to Paul shortly after Paul's conversion, yet he now hurt Paul deeply by choosing to eat with the Judaizers instead of the Gentiles. Eating with people showed an acceptance of them and their beliefs.

Before the Judaizers arrived, Cephas, Barnabas, and others had no difficulty eating with the Gentiles, but when the Jews arrived, they feared being seen as accepting the lifestyle and beliefs of the Gentiles, so they ceased eating with them and joined the Jewish party from Jerusalem. This was the source of Paul's anger. Although Paul does not tell us that the people from Jerusalem were Judaizers, he does hint at it when he states that Peter was afraid of the circumcised, that is, those who believed that circumcision was necessary for the followers of Jesus. In this statement, he is also rebuking the Galatians, who have also begun to accept the Mosaic practices.

Lectio Divina

Spend 8 to 10 minutes in silent contemplation of the following passage:

Peter is a saint, but he also demonstrates the weakness of being human, a weakness that most people striving to become saints must endure. Peter denied Christ during Jesus' passion, but he repented. After Jesus' ascension, he was willing to die for Christ when he refused an order to cease preaching about Christ or face death, yet he weakened when Judaizers came to Antioch. Paul does not tell us how Peter reacted to the reprimand, but following

Peter's history, we can suspect that he reflected on Paul's word and repented. So Peter's actions offer us an example of one who repents after making major mistakes. Despite his weakness, Peter showed strength and endurance, never allowing his failures to defeat him. Since the Church honors Peter as a saint, his life offers the message that no matter how often or badly we sin, God is a forgiving God who continually calls us to repentance and forgiveness.

On the other hand, Paul has the quality of a person totally dedicated to his or her beliefs. When he was a strict Jew, he worked tirelessly to persecute those he believed were destroying Judaism. Once he was converted to Christ, he dedicated his whole life to Christ, to the point that he could say that he no longer lived for himself, but for Christ. When the Judaizers arrived, Paul remained faithful to his commitment to the Gentile Christians, and he had no fear of challenging those who were too weak to live up to their commitments.

So Peter and Paul both stand as good examples for us as Christians today who desire to persevere in following Christ our Lord.

✠ *What can I learn from this passage?*

Day 2: Faith and Works (2:15–21)

Although Paul continues to report about his rebuke of Cephas, it is unlikely that he gave his lengthy speech at this time. He most likely reworked the situation to present his message in a concise and forceful manner. Paul reminds Cephas that both of them were born Jews, not Gentiles. Yet both men know that it is not the Law but faith in Christ that leads to justification. If their faith leads them to act more like Gentiles, does this mean that Christ is encouraging sin, since some consider the Gentile Christians as sinning in not accepting circumcision? Christ could never act in this fashion. Paul declares that they would be sinning if they sought to support the opposite of freedom in Christ, that is, if they were to support the Law. Paul states that he died to the Law and came to live for God. He considers a return to the Law to be a transgression for Peter as well as for himself.

Paul is stating that his whole life changed when he united himself with the crucified Christ. His life, although still a human life, now belongs to God through faith in Christ. The gift of Christ's love and life should not be seen as meaningless. If a person can be justified through the Law, then Christ had no reason for dying. The crux of Paul's argument is that the new life, given through Christ, cannot be ignored for the sake of the Law.

Lectio Divina

Spend 8 to 10 minutes in silent contemplation of the following passage:

Again, here Paul offers an example of total dedication. He had to totally deny his previous beliefs about the importance of the Mosaic Law and live with faith in Christ. To do this, God struck him blind, giving him an opportunity to reflect on the events of his conversion and what it meant for him. Conversion is difficult. This does not simply mean moving from one belief to another, but rather consists in being driven by a new belief over a previous one, and therefore changing one's attitude toward life. Paul reached a stage where he was willing to die for Christ. He knew that Christ was crucified and he was willing to be crucified for Christ. During his period of silence and darkness, Paul totally dedicated his life to Christ. Seeing how Paul could reflect on his new life, we can learn the value of contemplation. Conversion to Christ is not just a matter of saying we are committed, but it is a matter of deeply contemplating what our new commitments mean. These commitments can occur each day as we reflect more fully on the meaning of being dedicated to Christ, as Paul was.

✠ *What can I learn from this passage?*

Day 3: Christian Faith and Freedom (3:1–14)

Paul continues to speak strongly to the Galatians. He preached the message of Christ crucified to them, and this message led to their conversion. The only way Paul can explain their change of direction is to state that an evil spell has taken control of them. So he challenges them asking whether they received the gift of the Holy Spirit through faith in the gospel or through the Law. The implied answer is that they received the Spirit through faith. Paul then asks how they could be so foolish to exchange their faith for the Law. He repeats his questions in different ways. Has all been useless? Has observance of the Law or has faith prompted God to pour upon them the gift of the Spirit of many miracles?

Because it is the Judaizers who have turned the minds of the Galatians, Paul meets their arguments on their own ground. Even though he is writing to pagans, who are not as familiar with the Scriptures as the Jews, he chooses his examples from the Scriptures as the Judaizers must have done. He recalls the example of Abraham who, because of his faith, found favor with God before the Law and the covenant existed. Because the writers of the Scriptures, with God's inspiration, foresaw that it would be faith and not the Law that brought justification, they were able to say of Abraham that all nations would be blessed in him (Genesis 12:3). This justification occurred before the Law was given. From Paul's argument, one must conclude that a person who lives by faith shares in the same gift as Abraham.

In contrast, those who live by the Law are under its curse, because they must observe all of the Law. Because of this curse, no one can be justified by the Law. Justification comes through faith, and it is faith that makes a person just. Because the Law does not depend upon faith, a person cannot be justified by the Law.

The Book of Deuteronomy speaks of the curse of anyone who hung upon a cross (21:23). By accepting this curse, Jesus did away with the curse of the Law. Through Christ, the blessings that flowed upon Abraham through his faith can now come upon all the Gentiles. It is through this faith that the Gentiles are able to receive the Spirit.

Lectio Divina

Spend 8 to 10 minutes in silent contemplation of the following passage:

Paul realizes that true salvation does not come from following the Law with perfection, since the need to follow all the details of the Law still does not satisfy one's need to have faith. Paul shared faith in Jesus Christ to the Galatians, a faith free from the detailed traditions and practices of the Law, but he expresses his exasperation with them when he declares that they are foolish in seeking these details of the Law over faith in Jesus Christ. The true children of Abraham are those who live by faith, as Abraham himself did. He lived before God gave the Law to Moses. Faith in Jesus comes from the foolishness of the cross and brings salvation. For Paul, living under the Law is a curse, while living with faith in Christ crucified is a blessing.

✠ *What can I learn from this passage?*

Day 4: The Law and the Promise (3:15–18)

Paul references the legal customs of his day when he reminds his readers that a will cannot be changed or abolished once it becomes valid. In the same way, God's promises cannot be changed or abolished once they have been made. God made promises to Abraham and his "offspring." Abraham's offspring, as Paul explains, is Jesus Christ. Once God made these promises to Abraham and, through him, to Jesus, no law that came into existence later could invalidate these promises.

When Paul speaks of the number of years between the promise made to Abraham and the Law received by Moses as 430 years, he uses the reckoning found in some Greek readings of the Scriptures used in the synagogues during his time. The Hebrew Bible does not speak as clearly about the number of years between these two events as does the Greek. Paul states that one's inheritance comes either through the Law or through the promise, but not through both. Because God gave this gift to Abraham through the promise, long before the Law existed, the Law has no influence on it.

Lectio Divina

Spend 8 to 10 minutes in silent contemplation of the following passage:

> According to Paul, God's promise came to Abraham and his descendant, who is Jesus Christ. The Law is not the promise, and does not contradict the promise. The Law was there to prepare people for the coming of Christ, but once Christ came, then people have the call of living by faith in Jesus Christ who is the center of our faith. Knowing and living the message of Jesus Christ is living according to the promise God made to Abraham. According to Paul, through God's promise to Abraham, Christians have received the call to be God's people. Our law is the law of loving God, neighbor, and oneself. We often hear the expression, *What would Jesus do?* If we take the question seriously in difficult situations in our life, we would find this question to be extremely challenging.

✠ *What can I learn from this passage?*

Day 5: Promise Given Through Faith (3:19–22)

Realizing that he has divorced the Law from the promise, Paul must ask whether the Law has any relevance. He answers that the Law came into existence because of the transgressions of people. People sinned, and they needed some way to identify their sin; they needed someone or something to act as a type of "custodian" over their lives. This Law did not come directly from God, but through angels to a mediator who, we know, was Moses. In keeping with the theme of this letter, Paul reminds his readers that this Law was valid only until the coming of the offspring to whom the promise was given. Because of the coming of Jesus, we can no longer speak of a mediator, because Jesus is One with God. Jesus comes, not as the mediator of the promise, but as the fulfillment of the promise.

Paul declares that it is foolish to believe he is saying that the Law and the promise are opposed to each other. If, however, the Law had the same power to give life as the promise had, then the Law would lead to justification. A reading of the Scriptures (Old Testament) tells us that the Law did not have the power to give life, because the Scriptures show the constant power of sin in the world. When Paul asks why the Scriptures speak this way about sin, he seems to say that it is to help the believer recognize the great gift that comes through faith in Jesus Christ. The believer is able to share in the fulfillment of the promise.

Until the coming of Jesus Christ, the People of God had to follow the Law as a guide, or custodian. The coming of Christ brought about their justification and abolished the need for such a custodian. Now, through faith in Jesus Christ, they are sons and daughters of God. Through their baptism, they are clothed in Christ so that all are equal; there is no distinction between nations, social status, or gender. In Christ, all become one, and as true descendants of Abraham, all inherit the promise.

Lectio Divina

Spend 8 to 10 minutes in silent contemplation of the following passage:

Someone once said that human beings do not run away from things, but toward them. We all need a goal. People in abusive relationships often do not leave the relationship unless there is someone or something that they believe is able to help them. Jesus told us that *where our treasure is, there will our heart be*. In other words, what is important to us draws us in that direction. Athletes are willing to work for long hours, enduring every hardship in training because they have a goal. In this passage, Paul establishes a goal for us and invites us to reach toward that goal. As Christians who live by faith in Jesus Christ, we are heirs of the promise God made throughout salvation history.

Paul views the written law as a type of disciplinarian, and he views faith in Jesus as freedom from the law. He does not say that it is freedom from sin. Jesus does tell us what we should not do, but even more, Jesus tells us what we should do, namely to love one another. Jesus told his disciples, "As I have loved you, so you also should love one another" (John 13:34). Loving as Jesus loved is our goal. Paul tells us in this passage that all of us who were baptized into Christ Jesus have clothed ourselves in Christ, which means that we are asking ourselves what Christ would do if he had to act in a particular situation. The real goal of Christianity is not just to avoid sin, but to strive to be like Christ and to love as he loved. There is no longer Jew or Greek, slave or free, male or female, or any modern distinction we might make. We must strive for unity among Christians and recognize that Christ has called us all to be brothers and sisters.

✠ *What can I learn from this passage?*

Review Questions

1. Why does Paul become so angry when Peter leaves the table of the Gentile Christians to eat with the Jewish Christians?

2. How do Paul's words concerning freedom from the law and living by faith in Christ apply to us today?

3. What does Paul mean when he says that he does not live in the flesh, but that he lives in Christ?

4. How does Paul's reference to Abraham help him in convincing the Galatians that it is faith and not the law that brings justification?

5. Why is Paul able to say that we still live according to the covenant made with Abraham in the Old Testament?

6. How do we apply Paul's words of unity among all people to our lives today?

LESSON 7

Freedom for God's Children

GALATIANS 4—6

Let us not grow tired of doing good, for in due time we shall reap our harvest, if we do not give up (6:9).

Opening Prayer (SEE PAGE 20)

Context

Part 1: Galatians 4 Christ came to ransom us from the law. God sent the spirit of Christ into our hearts, meaning that we are no longer slaves but a child of God and an heir. Paul asks how the Galatians can choose to become slaves to the law again by reminding them that at one time they would have sacrificed all for him. Paul uses a reference to the labor pains of a woman who is giving birth to a child. He says that he is again in labor until Christ is formed in the Galatians, that is, until he is able to convert them to Christ. He uses the story of Hagar and Sarah to form an allegory in order to emphasize that those who follow Christ are the new children of the promise. Hagar gave birth to Ishmael who was not the child of promise, and Sarah gave birth to Isaac who was the child of promise, that is, the one who would carry on the promise God made to Abraham.

Part 2: Galatians 5—6 The argument Paul emphasized time and again is that faith is important, not circumcision; and one who accepts circumcision becomes bound by the Law. In this section, Paul denies he is still preaching circumcision. He states that love covers the whole law. If they learn to live by the Spirit, they will not seek to gratify the flesh. Instead, they must crucify the flesh and live in Christ by building one another up rather than destroying one another. As a community of Christ, they should have concern for one another, humbly serving the needs of all and doing good to one another. Writing in his own hand, Paul ends the letter by telling the Galatians that he wants his only boast to be in the cross of Jesus Christ.

PART 1: GROUP STUDY (GALATIANS 4)

Read aloud Galatians 4.

4:1–7 God's Free Children in Christ

Paul continues to refer to the legal practices of his day. An heir could have a large fortune coming to him or her, but as long as the heir was under age, a guardian or administrator was appointed as an administrator for the heir until the person reached a certain age. Despite the great wealth of the heir, he or she was no better than a slave. As a child or young adult, the heir had no say over the inheritance until the appointed time.

Paul applies this legal image to God's promises. Although the people were heirs of God's promises, they had no right to make full use of them, because the appointed time had not yet come, and they were still under age. Jesus came in the fullness of time to fulfill the promises made by God throughout the Old Testament. With the coming of Christ, we are no longer slaves but heirs with Christ. Jesus himself said, "I no longer call you slaves, because a slave does not know what his master is doing" (John 15:15). Those who have faith and knowledge of Jesus are friends of Jesus and heirs of the reign of God. With knowledge of the mystery of the death, resurrection, and ascension of Jesus, Christians are able to understand better the mystery of God's love more than the people of the Old Testament era.

When Paul states that God has sent the Son of God, he hints at the pre-existence of the Son. Jesus came into the world in the ordinary fashion, born of a woman and, as a good Jew, subject to Mosaic Law. In this way, he not only freed himself from that Law, but also freed all people from it, because all are called, through Christ, to become adopted sons and daughters of God. The proof of this call to be sons and daughters of God is heard in our prayer to God, whom we address as "Abba," or "Daddy." Since we no longer live under the slavery of the Law, we are no longer slaves, but sons and daughters of God. As such, we are heirs of the promise as God planned.

4:8–11 Protecting Freedom

Paul continues to show his surprise at how quickly the Galatians abandoned the message he shared with them. He reminds them that they were like slaves to false gods in the past, before they learned of the one, true God. He is astounded that they can turn back to these elements of the world of the false gods after they have known the true God in a most intimate way. Almost as an afterthought, Paul realizes that this intimate relationship is a gift from God, and he quickly adds that they allowed themselves to be known by God. After this initiative on the part of God, it is hard for Paul to understand how the Galatians could return to ceremonial observances. He is most likely referring to the Jewish observances of special days, months, seasons, and years set aside to honor God; observances that no longer bind them. When he hears of the Galatians' actions, Paul expresses his concern for them. In view of their desire to return to their old ways, Paul wonders if he has failed in his mission.

4:12–20 Appeal to Former Liberty

Paul asks the Galatians to become like him, to give up the Jewish practices. Just as he gave up these practices, so they should not allow themselves to become slaves to them. Paul tells the Galatians that they have done him no wrong (a possible reference to some action the Galatians believed hurt Paul). Paul reminds them that they accepted him despite some physical ailment that could have led them to reject him. He wonders what happened to their attitude. Because of their love for him, he explains that previously they would have done anything for him, even if it meant physical mutilation, such as plucking out their eyes. Paul asks if they have now rejected him because he has courageously spoken the truth to them.

Paul accuses the Judaizers (whom he does not mention by name) of showing interest in the Galatians, not for the sake of these Gentiles, but for the Judaizers themselves. Rather than showing interest for the sake of receiving some favors from Paul while he is present, it would be better if they showed interest in him for the right reasons—for Jesus Christ. Paul calls the Galatians his children and uses the image of a woman in labor when speaking of the pain they caused him. He uses the image of a woman in labor to teach about his love and desire for the Galatians to follow the ways of Christ. For he explains that after his labor pains of sharing Jesus Christ in the past, he feels he must experience these pains for them again. He ends this passage by expressing his frustration at not being able to speak directly with them.

4:21–31 An Allegory for Children of the Promise

Because the Galatians are so interested in being subject to the Law, Paul asks them if they truly understand what the Law says. He uses an example from Abraham's life. According to the Book of Genesis, Abraham had two sons, one by a slave girl named Hagar (16:15), who gave birth to Ishmael, and another by his true wife Sarah (21:2), who gave birth to Isaac. When Sarah realized she apparently would have no children, she gave Hagar to Abraham as a concubine, saying "perhaps I will have sons through her"(16:2). The act of giving a slave girl to one's husband with the hope of the slave girl having children was a custom in some areas in Abraham's era. The idea was that the sons of the slave girl would be considered the sons of the woman who owned the slave girl. Unfortunately for Sarah, Hagar, after giving birth to Ishmael, looked with disdain on Sarah, causing Sarah to be jealous of her. After the birth of Isaac, Sarah saw Ishmael playing with Isaac, and she told Abraham to cast out Hagar and Ishmael. At the prompting of God, a distraught Abraham cast the slave girl and her son into exile, but God promised to protect and bless Ishmael as the father of a great nation (see Genesis 16 and 21).

Paul states that he is making an allegory out of the story. He notes that the son of Hagar was born through the course of nature, that is, she was a girl of childbearing age. Sarah, however, gave birth to Isaac far beyond her childbearing age. Her son Isaac was born according to the promise made to Abraham, which made him the child of the promise. The two women stand for the two covenants, the covenant of the promise and the covenant of the Law. Hagar refers to the covenant made on Mount Sinai, the covenant of the Law, which gave birth to children in slavery. The Law made on Mount Sinai refers to the Law given to Moses on Mount Sinai in the desert during the Exodus. It is referred to as the Mosaic Law because the people believed that the Law came to them from God through Moses (see Exodus 19 and 20). Paul applies this Law to the Jerusalem of his own day, that is, those who were living under slavery of the Law. The Christian, however, lives in the freedom of faith and is the new Jerusalem, which Paul refers to as the Jerusalem above. This is a reference to the heavenly Jerusalem that has no earthly boundaries and is the throne of God.

Paul quotes from Isaiah the prophet (54:1) and applies the words to Sarah and the children of the promise. She is the barren one who breaks into song because she has many children, though the Book of Genesis does not mention that Sarah had any other children after Isaac. The reference was not intended to speak of Sarah's immediate children, but to the generation upon generation of people born through the line of Isaac. Paul informs the Galatians that they are the children of the promise, but they must realize that they will undergo persecution, just as the child of the promise was persecuted by Ishmael, the child of nature. In the book of Genesis, there is no report of Ishmael persecuting Isaac, but within Judaism there were such stories about this persecution, so Paul makes use of it here for the sake of the allegory. Paul, as a devout Jew, would have been familiar with these stories.

Just as Abraham is told by God to follow Sarah's directives and to cast out the slave girl and her son, Paul is telling the Galatians that they should follow the Scriptures and cast out those who live by the Law, whom Paul views as the slaves of his own day. They should remember that they are children of the promise, who are not bound to the Law.

Review Questions

1. What does it mean that we are a child of God and an heir according to the promise?

2. Why does Paul feel a need to warn the Galatians not to give away the freedom they have earned?

3. When Paul says that we live by faith and not be the law, is he saying that there is no law for those who follow Christ? Explain.

4. How does the allegory of Hagar and Sarah apply to our faith today?

Closing Prayer (SEE PAGE 20)

Pray the closing prayer now or after *lectio divina*.

Lectio Divina (SEE PAGE 11)

Relax your body and maintain a posture of prayer (back straight, eyes shut, feet flat on the floor). This exercise can take as long as you want, but in the context of this Bible study, 10 to 20 minutes should be sufficient.

The meditations that follow are provided only to help group participants use this prayer form, but note that *lectio* is intended to bring one to a place of prayerful contemplation where the Word of God speaks to the hearer from his or her heart. See page 11 for further instruction.

God's Free Children in Christ (4:1–7)

A man once said that the greatest compliment he received in life was the day when someone said to him that he was just like his father. He knew his father was a good man who showed love and concern for others, and a man whom others deeply admired. When we become heirs with Christ, we have the freedom to address God in an intimate manner as "Abba," which means "Daddy." It is not only the freedom that we should cherish, but it is the desire to be like Jesus, our spiritual model.

The Scriptures give us an image of Jesus' great love for us; and they also give us an understanding of the greatness of Mary's love. Both Jesus and Mary, intimately close to each other, could say as one to God, "Not my will, but yours be done." In becoming heirs with Christ, we do not find ourselves showered with millions of dollars but with an abundance of gifts from God. As heirs, we are meant to use these gifts as Jesus and Mary did, sharing them with others and using them to praise God. Jesus showed us how to live as a child and heir of God. Jesus became human, like us, redeemed us of our sins, called us friends and not slaves, and longed to have us reflect God in all we do. All of us, male and female, are made to the image and likeness of God. We think, we act, we pray, and, above all—as heirs—we are called to love as Jesus loved.

✠ *What can I learn from this passage?*

Protecting Freedom (4:8–11)

Alcoholism is a disease that afflicts a large percentage of people in our society. Those who know the strength of the disease and the over-whelming power of addiction develop great admiration for recovering alcoholics who go to meetings to help them remain sober and live a fruitful life. Unfortunately, there are some who lose the fight and re-turn to drink. Very often, their relatives will be perplexed, wondering why they abandoned the freedom of being sober for a liquid. They were able to control the disease for a period of time, and they later returned to their old ways.

Paul the Apostle preached to the Galatians about freedom from the law. He viewed them as slaves, as though they were addicted to the old ways, and he is astounded that they have returned to the law when they have a taste of freedom under Christ. For many Christians, sin can become an addictive force. Paul may have felt his mission to the Galatians was in vain, but he must remember that there were many Galatians who did not return to their old ways, just as there are many recovering alcohol-ics who have not returned to their old ways. For all of us, the old sinful ways of our life can be strong and alluring, but the new ways to live in the freedom of Christ's love make us the saints God wants us to be.

✠ *What can I learn from this passage?*

An Allegory for Children of the Promise (4:21–31)

A man at a spirituality conference told a surprising story about his conversion to Christ. He said that he grew up in a very strict home where every detail of his life was laid out for him. Later, as an adult Christian, he followed all rules rigidly and judged those who made exceptions to the rules. He would kneel up straight and stiff during worship, because he believed that this was what the Church asked of him. Every rule was followed to the letter, until the day his practice of piety and exactness fell apart.

As a minister of the Eucharist for the patients in a nearby hospital, he received a call on an afternoon to come to the hospital with Communion for a dying man. He promised that he would come after he finished the hour of adoration he vowed to make each day. As a result of his hour of prayer, he arrived at the hospital too late to administer Communion to the dying man who had now died. Suddenly, he said, it all hit him. He was so busy keeping the rules that he forgot to love Christ. His measurement was not compassion and love, but how well he kept every point of the rule.

He continued to say that he believed in the past that God must really love him for his exactness, but he suddenly realized that his gauge was how much God loved his punctuality rather than how much he loved God. He had become a slave to the rules instead of living in the freedom of loving Christ and following his example of love and compassion for others. He still kept the rules, but he would never again allow his rigid rules to stand in the way of living and loving as Christ did. Paul the Apostle had to confront those who felt that being holy meant following the rules of the Law rather than following the example and message of Jesus' life.

✠ *What can I learn from this passage?*

PART 2: INDIVIDUAL STUDY (GALATIANS 5—6)

Day 1: Living the Christian Life (5:1–12)

Paul draws some obvious conclusions for those who wish to live in the freedom of Christ. He reminds the Galatians that Christ already freed them once from the yoke of slavery, which is the Law. When Paul speaks of the freedom of Christ, he is not speaking of a freedom which allows the people to do whatever they wish, but a freedom from the dictates of the Law. In warning them not to become slaves a second time, Paul continues to view the Mosaic Laws and practices as a type of slavery. Once a person chooses circumcision in accord with Mosaic Law, that person must observe the entirety of the Law. To make a commitment to one area of the Law and not to other areas of the Law is not acceptable. The freedom brought by Jesus is useless to this person, because the person has not accepted Christ. Paul presents the bold truth that the person cannot follow the Law and Christ.

Righteousness comes not through the Law, but through faith in Jesus. Those who seek righteousness through the Law will not attain it, because they have cut themselves off from Christ. Whether or not a person is circumcised has no bearing on righteousness. After ranting against circumcision, Paul seems to be allowing the Galatians to choose to be circumcised, but Paul is saying that they cannot accept only part of the Law. If they accept circumcision as an acceptance of the Law, then they are slaves to the Law. So it is not circumcision itself which is wrong, but the ritual that commits a person to the Law through circumcision.

Paul continues to wonder at the sudden and unexpected change in the progress being made by the Galatians, and he wonders who has been influential enough to bring about this change. He knows that it did not come from God, and he curses the person who has influenced the Galatians in this matter. Despite this disrupting influence, Paul still has confidence that his readers will not succumb to this enticement.

Some have apparently preached that Paul supported the idea of circumcision. Paul asks why he is still under attack by the Judaizers if this is true. If Paul had agreed to follow the Law, then he could abandon his preaching of the cross of Jesus that stands as a "stumbling block" for so many. Paul's anger reaches such a height that he sarcastically wishes that those who are causing all the trouble would castrate themselves.

Lectio Divina

Spend 8 to 10 minutes in silent contemplation of the following passage:

Jesus himself confronted some of the Jewish rituals, especially the dietary laws. The dietary laws of Israel forbade the eating of certain foods, but Jesus challenged the laws. At one point, he said, "Nothing that enters one from outside can defile that person; but the things that come out from within are what defile" (Mark 7:15). Paul recognizes that a person who accepts the Mosaic Laws must accept all the laws, including dietary laws. For Paul, this is a form of slavery to the law. Jesus later clarifies his statement. He says, "From within people, from their hearts, come evil thoughts, unchastity, theft, murder, adultery, greed, malice, deceit, licentiousness, envy, blasphemy, arrogance, folly. All these evils come from within, and they defile." As Paul emphasizes in Galatians, following Jesus in faith is not a license to sin, but it is freedom from many of the rituals and practices of the Mosaic Law. Those who live in the freedom of Christ show love for God, neighbor, and self. The sins listed by Jesus are sins against love of God, neighbor, and self.

✠ *What can I learn from this passage?*

Day 2: Freedom for Service (5:13–26)

Lest someone thinks that Paul is saying that a person may live by faith and act in whatever manner he or she wishes, he states that justification comes through faith, which is expressed by love. A person of faith lives a life of love which calls for service to one another. Love is the fulfillment of the law, love of neighbor as oneself. When Paul speaks of the law in this passage, he is not speaking about the Mosaic Law, but the law that covers all people. If they continue to bicker with one another, they will soon destroy one another.

Paul uses the common image of the Spirit versus the flesh. He is not speaking of the body and soul here, but of the world of God (the Spirit) and the world of sin (flesh). Since the Spirit and the flesh are opposed to each other, they are in continual conflict. Paul sees such a battle as the cause for a person to perform some deeds they do not wish to perform. The person who lives by the Spirit lives in union with Christ, without the Law. In speaking of the war between the flesh and the Spirit, Paul names deeds that flow from both. These deeds were taken from several preset lists used by missionaries in the early Church. Paul states that the sins of the flesh are obvious: sexual sins (such as fornication and impurity), false worship (such as idolatry and sorcery), social sins (such as jealousy and anger), and sins of overindulgence (such as drunkenness and carousing). Those who practice these evil actions will not inherit the kingdom of God.

Paul next lists the fruit of the Spirit as love, joy, peace, patience, kindness, generosity, faithfulness, gentleness, and self-control. Those who practice these deeds have no need for the Law. He states that those who belong to Christ have crucified their flesh with its passions and desires. True freedom consists of crucifying the flesh and its power to enslave a person and living by the Spirit without any need to boast, confront another, or become jealous. Just as Jesus found life and freedom when the Roman soldiers crucified him in the flesh, so his followers will find freedom when they crucify their passions and desires.

Lectio Divina

Spend 8 to 10 minutes in silent contemplation of the following passage:

Paul declares that the flesh has desires against the Spirit, which means that even for those who dedicate themselves to freedom in Christ must still endure temptation. Saint Gregory writes that Saint Benedict had such an overwhelming temptation of the flesh that he had to throw himself into briars and nettles to distract himself from the temptation. As holy and dedicated as Saint Benedict was, the Spirit within him was still at war with the flesh. Paul uses an apt phrase in Galatians when he says that "those who belong to Christ have crucified their flesh with its passions and desires" (5:24). We may not be called to crucify our flesh to the extent that Benedict did, but we realize that overcoming temptations becomes such a struggle at times that it is almost like a crucifixion in Spirit.

✠ *What can I learn from this passage?*

Day 3: Life in the Community of Christ (6:1–10)

In the opening words of this passage, Paul seems to be addressing the Galatians who have withstood the enticements of the Judaizers who are attempting to bring all Christians to accept the Mosaic practices along with their faith in Christ. He urges them to correct the sinner with gentleness while, at the same time, protecting themselves against any temptations to sin. As members of a true Christian community, they must learn to bear each other's burdens. Paul sees this as a sign that the Christian is truly fulfilling the law of Christ. No one should be deceived into thinking that he or she is better than others. All must bear their own burdens, and, if they are satisfied that they have done well, then they should boast within themselves and not burden their neighbor with their boasting. Paul continually makes reference to the idea of boasting in his letters. He states that an individual has little reason to boast, since, he believes, all good actions are performed through Christ with the guidance of the Spirit.

Those who taught in the early Church had to depend on their "students" for support for their ministry. Paul reminds his readers about this practice, telling them that they should share good things with their instructors. These instructors may be compared to catechists who are instructing the Galatians about Jesus and his message. Paul tells them that God cannot be fooled. The final reward of individuals depends on what they sow during their lives. Those who sow in the flesh will reap the rewards of the flesh—namely, corruption—while those who sow in the Spirit will receive the rewards of the Spirit—that is, eternal life. Paul encourages his readers not to weaken in doing good, because the time of harvest, the Second Coming, will arrive in due time. During this time of waiting, we should do good to all, but especially to those who belong to the family of the faith.

Lectio Divina

Spend 8 to 10 minutes in silent contemplation of the following passage:

Paul has great concern for those who belong to the family of Christ. He urges his readers to do well for all people, and especially those who belong to the family of faith. A pastor once told his associate that he may be away for a short time because he was donating his kidney to someone. The associate naturally asked him if the recipient were a relative, and the pastor admitted that he did not know the person. He simply placed his name on the list, allowed them to test him, and offered his kidney to whomever needed it. His response to his associate was, "After all, we are brothers and sisters in Christ."

This pastor brought to the extreme the call to love those who belong to the family of faith. He believed that all people belonged to Christ's family, and he was making an offering that most of us would never dream of making. By his offering, he was teaching a lesson. Paul said that a person will reap what the person sows. With his attitude and his offering of his kidney, the belief of all of us is that the pastor will reap a great reward before God. God may not expect us to have the degree of gift giving the pastor had for the members of the family of Christ, but God does expect us to share our gifts with others in some manner. As Paul says, "while we have the opportunity, let us do good to all" (Galatians 6:10).

✠ *What can I learn from this passage?*

Day 4: Conclusion (6:11–18)

Paul often had a secretary write his letters for him. When he did this, he would write the last section of the letter in his own hand to prove to those to whom he wrote that the letter actually came from him. Paul tells the Galatian readers that he is writing this last section to them in his own hand. The reference to writing in large letters could be implied to mean that his eyesight was failing, or that he believed his own handwriting not to be as neat as that of his scribe.

In this section, he summarizes much of what he has said in his letter. He accuses some among them (the Judaizers?) of trying to force the Galatians to accept circumcision, not for any spiritual good, but for the sake of approval from other Judaizers. Paul further accuses them of trying to escape the message of the cross of Jesus Christ, and of not carrying out the Law, despite their circumcision. Since the Jews were accepted in Galatia, some believers in Christ may be accepting circumcision to avoid those who were persecuting uncircumcised Christians. The Judaizers are simply looking for the Galatian Christians to accept the external observance of circumcision so that they can boast of the number of converts to the Law. For Paul, circumcision or the lack of circumcision means nothing. What is important is living in the new creation brought about by Jesus.

Paul again speaks of his boast—the cross of Jesus Christ. The cross does not allow him to boast about himself, but to boast about the effect of the cross on him. Through the cross, the world has died (was crucified) for Paul, and Paul has died (has been crucified) to the world. The world no longer has anything to offer Paul, who is now a new creation in Christ. This could be an admission on Paul's part that he is ready for death whenever it comes.

As the letter draws to a close, Paul wishes the usual peace and mercy to those who are faithful to his message. He refers to those who are following the rule of the gospel as the "Israel of God." He abruptly begs the Galatians not to persist in causing him trouble, reminding them that he has already borne many of the labors and sufferings of a Christian disciple. He calls the evident signs of this difficult ministry "the marks of Jesus" on his body. In Paul's day, slave owners often had their slaves branded to identify who owned them. Some view Paul's reference to the marks of Jesus in his flesh as the stigmata, which refers to the wounds of Christ crucifixion showing on the hands and side of saintly people. Paul may instead be referring to the marks in his flesh caused by his floggings and stoning when he was being persecuted for his message about Christ; a sign that he belongs to Christ.

The letter ends briefly and formally as Paul wishes the grace of the Lord Jesus Christ be with the Galatians. He adds an "Amen" to his final wishes.

Lectio Divina

Spend 8 to 10 minutes in silent contemplation of the following passage:

Paul's boast is that he bears the wounds of Christ in his body. His reason for boasting is not to tell people how wonderful and strong his faith is, but to tell the world that he is a slave and a fool for Christ. His wish is that others will see his faith and imitate his spirit.

As Christians, we bear the name of Christ as part of our identity. And as Christ's followers, the marks of our faith may not appear in our flesh, but it is the hope that they will appear in our manner of life. The dedication and courage of Paul is indeed a challenge for us who would wish to commit ourselves to Christ as totally as Paul did. If we have any reason to boast, our boasting like that of Paul is to boast in the love which God shows us. It is foolish to boast about one's skills or accomplishments, since they all come from God. In Luke's Gospel, we learn that we should have an attitude of a servant of the Lord who can say after performing tasks well, "We are unprofitable servants; we have done what we were obliged to do" (17:10). We can rejoice in the gifts God has given to us and we can leave the boasting up to God.

✠ *What can I learn from this passage?*

Review Questions

1. Why does Paul believe that living by the Mosaic Law takes away freedom from the Galatian Christians?

2. How is circumcision a stumbling block for faith in Christ?

3. What law of Christ replaces the Mosaic Law?

4. What does Paul mean when he contrasts the Spirit with the flesh?

5. What does it mean to live in a community of love?

6. Why does Paul insist on writing the last words of the letter in his own handwriting?